Curious Epitaphs:
Collected from the
Graveyards
of Great Britain
and Ireland

Also from Westphalia Press
westphaliapress.org

The Idea of the Digital University

Criminology Confronts Cultural Change

Eight Decades in Syria

Avant-Garde Politician

Socrates: An Oration

Strategies for Online Education

Conflicts in Health Policy

Material History and Ritual Objects

Jiu-Jitsu Combat Tricks

Opportunity and Horatio Alger

Careers in the Face of Challenge

Bookplates of the Kings

Collecting American Presidential Autographs

Misunderstood Children

Original Cables from the Pearl Harbor Attack

Social Satire and the Modern Novel

The Amenities of Book Collecting

Trademark Power

A Definitive Commentary on Bookplates

James Martineau and Rebuilding Theology

Royalty in All Ages

The Middle East: New Order or Disorder?

The Man Who Killed President Garfield

Chinese Nights Entertainments: Stories from Old China

Understanding Art

Homeopathy

The Signpost of Learning

Collecting Old Books

The Boy Chums Cruising in Florida Waters

The Thomas Starr King Dispute

Salt Water Game Fishing

Lariats and Lassos

Mr. Garfield of Ohio

The Wisdom of Thomas Starr King

The French Foreign Legion

War in Syria

Naturism Comes to the United States

Water Resources: Iniatives and Agendas

Designing, Adapting, Strategizing in Online Education

Feeding the Global South

The Design of Life: Development from a Human Perspective

Curious Epitaphs
Collected from the Graveyards of Great Britain and Ireland
with Biographical, Genealogical, and Historical Notes

by William Andrews

WESTPHALIA PRESS
An Imprint of Policy Studies Organization

Curious Epitaphs: Collected from the Graveyards
of Great Britain and Ireland
All Rights Reserved © 2016 by Policy Studies Organization

Westphalia Press
An imprint of Policy Studies Organization
1527 New Hampshire Ave., NW
Washington, D.C. 20036
info@ipsonet.org

ISBN-10: 1-63391-515-8
ISBN-13: 978-1-63391-515-2

Cover design by Jeffrey Barnes:
jbarnesbook.design

Daniel Gutierrez-Sandoval, Executive Director
PSO and Westphalia Press

OLD SCARLETT, THE PETERBOROUGH SEXTON.

PRINTED BY

CHARLES HENRY BARNWELL, HULL.

CURIOUS EPITAPHS

COLLECTED FROM THE GRAVEYARDS OF GREAT BRITAIN AND IRELAND,

WITH

Biographical, Genealogical, and Historical Notes.

BY

WILLIAM ANDREWS, F.R.H.S.,

Member of the Derbyshire Archæological and Natural History Society.
Secretary of the Hull Literary Club.
Local Secretary of the National Society for Preserving the Memorials of the Dead.
Author of "Historic Romance," "Historic Yorkshire,"
"Punishments in the Olden Time," "Book of Oddities,"
"History of the Dunmow Flitch," etc.

✚✚✚✚✚✚✚✚

LONDON:
HAMILTON, ADAMS, AND COMPANY.

TO

WILLIAM, DUKE OF DEVONSHIRE, K.G.,

ETC., ETC.,

THIS BOOK IS RESPECTFULLY DEDICATED BY

HIS GRACE'S KIND PERMISSION,

AS A TOKEN OF GRATITUDE FOR ENCOURAGEMENT AND

FAVOURS BESTOWED

WHEN THEY WERE MOST NEEDED.

W. A.

Preface.

FOR many years I have collected curious epitaphs, and in this volume I offer the result of my gleanings. An attempt is herein made to furnish a book, not compiled from previously published works, but a collection of curious inscriptions copied from gravestones. Some of the chapters have appeared under my name in *Chambers's Journal, Illustrated Sporting and Dramatic News, Newcastle Courant, People's Journal,* (Dundee), *Press News,* and other publications. I have included a Bibliography of Epitaphs, believing that it will be useful to those who desire to obtain more information on the subject than is presented here. I have not seen any other bibliography of this class of literature, and as a first attempt it must be incomplete. In compiling it I have had the efficient aid of Mr. W. G. B. Page, of the Hull Subscription Library, who has also prepared the Index.

I must tender my thanks to the following friends for their valued assistance: Mrs. Geo. Linnæus Banks, author of the "Manchester Man," Mr. W. G. Fretton, F.S.A., Mr. Walter Hamilton, F.R.G.S., Mr. Jno. H. Leggott, F.R.H.S., Rev. R. V. Taylor, B.A., Mr. H. Vickery, and others whose names appear in the following pages.

In conclusion, I hope that this book will merit from readers and reviewers a similar welcome to that granted to my former works; in that case I shall have every reason to be satisfied with my pleasant labour.

WILLIAM ANDREWS.

Hull Literary Club,
       October 1st, 1883.

Contents.

EPITAPHS ON PARISH CLERKS AND SEXTONS	1
TYPOGRAPHICAL EPITAPHS	14
EPITAPHS ON SPORTSMEN	21
EPITAPHS ON TRADESMEN	33
BACCHANALIAN EPITAPHS	54
EPITAPHS ON SOLDIERS AND SAILORS	65
PUNNING EPITAPHS	84
EPITAPHS ON MUSICIANS AND ACTORS	90
EPITAPHS ON NOTABLE PERSONS	108
MISCELLANEOUS EPITAPHS	150
BIBLIOGRAPHY OF EPITAPHS	157
INDEX	173

Curious Epitaphs.

EPITAPHS ON PARISH CLERKS AND SEXTONS.

AMONGST the most curious of the many peculiar epitaphs which are to be found in the quiet resting-places of the departed are those placed to the memory of parish clerks and sextons. We have noted at various times, and at different places, many strange specimens, a few of which we think will entertain our readers.

In the churchyard of Crayford is a grave-stone bearing the following inscription :—

Here lieth the body
OF
PETER ISNELL,
Thirty years clerk of this Parish.
He lived respected as a pious and mirthful man, and died on his way to church to assist at a wedding,
On the 31st day of March, 1811,
Aged 70 years.

The inhabitants of Crayford have raised this stone to his cheerful memory, and as a tribute to his long and faithful services.

> The life of this clerk, just three score and ten,
> Nearly half of which time he had sung out "Amen;"
> In youth he was married, like other young men,
> But his wife died one day, so he chanted "Amen."
> A second he took, she departed—what then?
> He married and buried a third with "Amen."
> Thus his joys and his sorrows were treble, but then
> His voice was deep bass, as he sung out "Amen."
> On the horn he could blow as well as most men;
> So his horn was exalted to blowing "Amen."
> But he lost all his wind after three score and ten,
> And here, with three wives, he awaits till again
> The trumpet shall rouse him to sing out "Amen."

In addition to being parish clerk, Frank Raw, of Selby, Yorkshire, was a grave-stone cutter, for we are told :—

> Here lies the body of poor Frank Raw,
> Parish clerk and grave-stone cutter,
> And this is writ to let you know
> What Frank for others used to do,
> Is now for Frank done by another.

The next epitaph, placed to the memory of a parish clerk and bellows-maker, was formerly in the old church of All Saints, Newcastle-on-Tyne :—

> Here lies Robert Wallas,
> The King of Good Fellows,

> Clerk of All-Hallows,
> And maker of bellows.

On a slate head-stone, near the south porch of Bingham Church, Nottinghamshire, is inscribed:—

> Beneath this stone lies Thomas Hart,
> Years fifty eight he took the part
> Of Parish Clerk: few did excel.
> Correct he read and sung so well;
> His words distinct, his voice so clear,
> Till eighteen hundred and fiftieth year.
> Death cut the brittle thread, and then
> A period put to his Amen.
> At eighty-two his breath resigned,
> To meet the fate of all mankind;
> The third of May his soul took flight
> To mansions of eternal light.
> The bell for him with awful tone
> His body summoned to the tomb.
> Oh! may his sins be all forgiv'n
> And Christ receive him into heav'n.

In the same county, from the churchyard of Ratcliffe on Soar, we have a curious epitaph to the memory of Robert Smith, who died in 1782, aged 82 years:—

> Fifty-five years it was, and something more,
> Clerk of this parish he the office bore,
> And in that space, 'tis awful to declare,
> Two generations buried by him were!

In a note by Mr. Llewllynn Jewitt, F.S.A., we are told that with the clerkship of Bakewell church, the "vocal powers" of its holders, appear to have been to some extent hereditary, if we may judge by the inscriptions recording the deaths and the abilities of two members of the family of Roe which are found on grave-stones in the churchyard there. The first of these, recording the death of Samuel Roe, is as under :—

> To
> The memory of
> SAMUEL ROE,
> Clerk
> Of the Parish Church of Bakewell,
> Which office
> He filled thirty-five years
> With credit to himself
> And satisfaction to the Inhabitants.
> His natural powers of voice,
> In clearness, strength, and sweetness
> Were altogether unequalled.
> He died October 31st, 1792,
> Aged 70 years.
>
> | | died | aged |
> |----------------------|------|------|
> | Sarah his third wife | 1811 | 77 |
> | Charles their son | 1810 | 52 |

He had three wives, Millicent, who died in 1745, aged 22 ; Dorothy, who died 1754, aged 28 ; and Sarah, who survived him and died in 1811, at the age of 77. A grave-stone records the death of his first two wives as follows, and the third is commemorated in the above inscription.

> Millicent,
> Wife of Saml Roe,
> She died Sepr 16th, 1745, aged 22.

Dorothy,
Wife of Saml Roe,
She died Novr 13th, 1754, aged 28.

Respecting the above-mentioned Samuel Roe, a contributor to the *Gentleman's Magazine* wrote, on February 13th, 1794:

" Mr. Urban,

" It was with much concern that I read the epitaph upon Mr. Roe, in your last volume, p. 1192. Upon a little tour which I made in Derbyshire, in 1789, I met with that worthy and very intelligent man at Bakewell, and, in the course of my antiquarian researches there, derived no inconsiderable assistance from his zeal and civility. If he did not possess the learning of his namesake, your old and valuable correspondent, I will venture to declare that he was not less influenced by a love and veneration for antiquity, many proofs of which he had given by his care and attention to the monuments in the church, which were committed to his charge; for he united the characters of sexton, clerk, singing-master, will-maker, and school-master. Finding that I was quite alone, he requested permission to wait upon me at the inn in the evening, urging, as a reason for this request, that he must be exceedingly gratified by the conversation of a gentleman who could read the characters upon the monument of Vernon, the founder of Haddon House, a treat he had not met with for many years. After a very pleasant gossip we parted, but not till my honest friend had, after some apparent struggle, begged of me to indulge him with my name."

To his careful attention is to be attributed the preservation of the curious Vernon and other monuments in the church, over which in some instances he placed wooden framework to keep off the rough hands and rougher knives of the boys and young men of the congregation. He also watched with special care over the Wendesley tomb, and even took careful rubbings of the inscriptions.

While speaking of this Mr. Roe, it may be well to put the readers of this work in possession of an interesting fact in connection with the name of Roe, or Row. The writer above, in his letter to Mr. Urban, says, " If he did not possess the learning of his namesake, your old and valued correspondent," &c. By this he means " T Row," whose contributions to the *Gent's. Mag.* were very numerous and interesting. The writer under this signature was the Rev. Samuel Pegge, rector of Whittington, and the letters forming this pseudonym were the initials of the words, T [he] R [ector] O [f] W [hittington].

Philip Roe, who succeeded his father (Samuel Roe) as parish clerk of Bakewell, was his son by his third wife. He was born in 1763, and succeeded his father in full parochial honours in 1792, having, we believe, for some time previously acted as his deputy. He died in 1815, aged 52 years, and was buried with the other members of the family. The following curious inscripton appears on his grave-stone :—

> Erected
> In remembrance of
> PHILIP ROE
> *who died 12th September,* 1815
> AGED 52 YEARS.
>
> The vocal Powers here let us mark
> Of Philip our late Parish Clerk
> In Church none ever heard a Layman
> With a clearer Voice say "Amen !"
> Who now with Hallelujahs Sound
> Like Him can make the Roofs rebound ?
> The Choir lament his Choral Tones
> The Town—so soon Here lie his Bones.
> "Sleep undisturb'd within thy peaceful shrine
> Till Angels wake thee with such notes as thine."
>
> Also of SARAH his wife
> who departed this life on the
> 24th of January 1817
> aged 51 years.

Our genial friend, Cuthbert Bede, B.A., author of "Verdant Green," tells us, "As a boy I often attended the service at Belbroughton Church, Worcestershire, where the parish clerk was Mr. Osborne, tailor. His family had there been parish clerks and tailors since the time of Henry the Eighth, and were lineally descended from William FitzOsborne, who, in the twelfth century, had been deprived by Ràlph FitzHerbert of his right to the manor of Bellem, in the parish of Belbroughton. Often have I stood in the picturesque churchyard of Wolverley, Worcestershire, by the grave of its old parish clerk, whom I well remember, old Thomas Worrall, the inscription on whose monument is as follows :—

> Sacred to the Memory of
> THOMAS WORRALL,
> Parish Clerk of Wolverley for a period of forty-seven years.
> Died A.D. 1854, February 23rd.
> Aged 76 years.
>
> " He served with faithfulness in humble sphere,
>   As one who could his talent well employ.
>   ⸢Hope that when Christ his Lord shall reappear,
>   He may be bidden to his Master's joy.
>
> This tombstone was erected to the memory of the deceased by a few of the parishioners in testimony of his worth.
>
> April, 1855.   Charles R. Somers Cocks, vicar.

It may be noted of this worthy parish clerk that, with the exception of a week or two before his death, he was never once absent from his Sunday and week-day duties in the forty-seven years during which he held office. He succeeded his father, James Worrall, who died in 1806, aged seventy-nine, after being parish clerk of Wolverley for thirty years. His tombstone, near to that of his son, was erected " to record his worth both in his public and private character, and as a mark of personal esteem—h. l. F. H. & W. C. p. c." I am told that these initials stand for F. Hurtle and the Rev. William Callow, and that the latter was the author of the following lines inscribed on the monument, which are well worth quoting :—

> If courtly bards adorn each statesman's bust,
> And strew their laurels o'er each warrior's dust
> Alike immortalise, as good and great,
> Him who enslaved as him who saved the state,
> Surely the muse (a rustic minstrel) may
> Drop one wild flower upon a poor man's clay ;
> This artless tribute to his mem'ry give
> Whose life was such as heroes seldom live.
> In worldly knowledge, poor indeed his store—
> He knew the village and he scarce knew more.
> The worth of heavenly truth he justly knew—
> In faith a Christian, and in practice too.
> Yes, here lies one, excel him ye who can ;
> Go ! imitate the virtues of that man !"

First amongst notable sextons is the name of Old Scarlett, who died July 2, 1591, at the good old age of ninety-eight, and occupied for a long time the position as sexton of Peterborough Cathedral. He buried two generations of his fellow-creatures. A portrait of him, placed at the west end of that noble church, has perpetuated his fame, and caused him to be introduced in effigy in various publications. Dr. Robert Chambers in his entertaining work, the " Book of Days," writes : " And what a lively effigy—short, stout, hardy, and self-complacent, perfectly satisfied, and perhaps even proud, of his profession, and content to be exhibited with all its insignia about him ! Two queens had passed through his hands into that bed which gives a lasting rest to queens and to peasants alike. An officer of Death, who had so long defied his principal, could not but have made some impression on the minds of bishop, dean, prebends, and other magnates of the Cathedral, and hence, as we may suppose, the erection of this lively portraiture of the old man, which is believed to have been only once renewed since it was first put up. Dr. Dibdin, who last copied it, tells us that ' Old Scarlett's jacket and trunkhose are of a brownish red, his stockings blue, his shoes black, tied with blue ribbons, and the soles of his feet red. The cap upon his head is red, and so also is the ground of the coat armour.' "

The following lines below h:s portrait are charcter-istic of his age :—

> You see old Scarlett's picture stand on hie ;
> But at your feet here doth his body lye.
> His gravestone doth his age and death-time show,
> His office by heis token [s] you may know.
> Second to none for strength and sturdy lymm,
> A scare-babe mighty voice, with visage grim ;
> He had inter'd two queenes within this place,
> And this townes householders in his life's space
> Twice over ; but at length his own time came
> What he for others did, for him the same
> Was done : no doubt his soule doth live for aye,
> In heaven, though his body clad in clay.

The first of the queens interred by Scarlett was Catherine, the divorced wife of Henry VIII, who died in 1535, at Kimbolton Castle, in Huntingdonshire.

The second was Mary Queen of Scots, who was beheaded at Fotheringay in 1587, and first interred here, though subsequently transported to Westminster Abbey.

Our next example is from Bingley, Yorkshire :—

In memory of Hezekiah Briggs, who died August 5th, 1844, in the 80th year of his age. He was sexton at this church 43 years, and interred upwards of 7000 corpses.

[Here the names of his wife and several children are given.]

Here lies an old ringer, beneath the cold clay,
Who has rung many peals both for serious and gay ;
Through Grandsire and Trebles with ease he could range,
Till death called a Bob, which brought round the last change.

        For all the village came to him
        When they had need to call ;
        His counsel free to all was given,
        For he was kind to all.

        Ring on, ring on, sweet Sabbath bell,
        Still kind to me thy matins swell,
        And when from earthly things I part,
        Sigh o'er my grave, and lull my heart.

An upright stone in the burial ground at Hartwith Chapel, in Nidderdale, Yorkshire, bears the following inscription :—

In memory of William Darnbrough, who for the last forty years of his life was sexton of this chapel. He died October 3rd, 1846, in the one hundreth year of his age,

" Thou shalt go to thy fathers in peace ; thou shalt be buried in a good old age."—*Genesis* xv. 15.

> The graves around for many a year
> Were dug by him who slumbers here,—
> Till worn with age, he dropped his spade,
> And in the dust his bones were laid.
>
> As he now, mouldering, shares the doom
> Of those he buried in the tomb ;
> So shall he, too, with them arise,
> To share the judgment of the skies.

An examination of Pateley Bridge Church registers proves that Darnbrough was 102 years of age.

An epitaph from Saddleworth, Yorkshire, tells us :—

Here was interred the body of John Broadbent, Sexton, who departed this life, August 3rd, 1769, in the 73rd year of his age.

> Forty-eight years, strange to tell,
> He bore the bier and toll'd the bell,
> And faithfully discharged his trust,
> In "earth to earth" and "dust to dust."
>   Cease to lament,
>   His life is spent,
> The grave is still his element ;
> His old friend Death knew 'twas his sphere,
> So kindly laid the sexton here.

At Rothwell, near Leeds, an old sexton is buried in the church porch. A monumental inscription runs thus :—

In memory of Thomas Flockton, Sexton 59 years, buried 23rd day of February, 1783, aged 78 years.

> Here lies within this porch so calm,
>   Old Thomas. Pray sound his knell,
> Who thought no song was like a psalm—
>   No music like a bell.

At Darlington, there is a Latin epitaph over the remains of Richard Preston, which has been freely translated as follows :—

> Under this marble are depos'd
>   Poor Preston's sad remains.
> Alas! too true for light-rob'd jest
>   To sing in playful strains.
>
> Ye dread possessors of the grave,
>   Who feed on others' woe,
> Abstain from Richard's small remains,
>   And grateful pity shew ;
>
> For many a weighty corpse he gave
>   To you with liberal hand ;
> Then sure his little body may
>   Some small respect command,

The gravestone bears the date of 1765.

Further examples might be included, but we have given sufficient to show the varied and curious epitaphs placed to the memory of parish clerks and sextons.

TYPOGRAPHICAL EPITAPHS.

THE trade of printer is rich in technical terms available for the writer of epitaphs, as will be seen in the following examples.

Our first inscription is from St. Margaret's Church, Westminster, placed in remembrance of England's benefactor, the first English printer:—

To the memory of
WILLIAM CAXTON,
who first introduced into Great Britain
the Art of Printing;
And who, A.D. 1477 or earlier, exercised that art in the
Abbey of Westminster.
This Tablet,
In remembrance of one to whom the literature of this
country is so largely indebted, was raised,
anno Domini MDCCCXX.,
by the Roxburghe Club,
Earl Spencer, K.G., President.

The next is in memory of one Edward Jones, *ob.* 1705-6, *æt.* 53. He was the "Gazette" Printer of the Savoy, and the following epitaph was appended to an elegy, entitled, "The Mercury Hawkers in Mourning," and published on the occasion of his death :—

> Here lies a Printer, famous in his time,
> Whose life by lingering sickness did decline.
> He lived in credit, and in peace he died,
> And often had the chance of Fortune tried.
> Whose smiles by various methods did promote
> Him to the favour of the Senate's vote;
> And so became, by National consent,
> The only Printer of the Parliament.
> Thus by degrees, so prosp'rous was his fate,
> He left his heirs a very good estate.

Another is on a noted printer and bookseller in his day, Jacob Tonson, who died in 1735 :—

> The volume of his life being finished, here is the end of Jacob Tonson. Weep, authors, and break your pens; your Tonson, effaced from the book, is no more; but print the last inscription on this last page of death, for fear that, delivered to the press of the grave, he, the Editor, should want a title. Here lies a bookseller, the leaf of his life being finished, awaiting a new edition, augmented and corrected.

The celebrated Dr. Benjamin Franklin imitated the above, and designed it for himself :—

> The body of B. Franklin, Printer, like the cover of an old book, its contents torn out, and stripped of its lettering and gilding, lies here, food for worms. But the work shall not be wholly lost, for it will, as he believed, appear once more, in a new and more perfect edition, corrected and amended by the Author He was born Jan. 6, 1706. Died ———, 17—. B.F.

Franklin died on the 17th of April, 1790, aged eighty-four years. After the death of this sturdy patriot and sagacious writer, the following singular sentiment was inscribed to his memory :—

> Benjamin Franklin, the * of his profession ; the type of honesty ; the ! of all ; and although the ☞ of death put a . to his existence, each § of his life is without a ||.

On a plain, flat slab in the burial-ground of Christ-church, Philadelphia, the following simple inscription appears over the remains of the good man and his worthy wife :—

Benjamin } Franklin.
Deborah

February, 1790.

The pun on the supersession of an old edition by a new and revised one, has often been worked out, as in the following example, which is that of the Rev. John Cotton, who died in New England, in 1652 :—

> A living, breathing Bible ; tables where
> Both covenants at large engraven were ;
> Gospel and law in his heart had each its column,
> His head an index to the sacred volume !
> His very name a title-page ; and, next,
> His life a commentary on the text.
> Oh, what a moment of glorious worth,
> When in a new edition he comes forth !
> Without errata, we may think 'twill be,
> In leaves and covers of Eternity.

A notable epitaph was that of George Faulkner, the alderman and printer, of Dublin, who died in 1775 :

> Turn, gentle stranger, and this urn revere,
> O'er which Hibernia saddens with a tear.

> Here sleeps George Faulkner, printer, once so dear
> To humorous Swift, and Chesterfield's gay peer;
> So dear to his wronged country and her laws;
> So dauntless when imprisoned in her cause;
> No alderman e'er graced a weightier board,
> No wit e'er joked more freely with a lord.
> None could with him in anecdotes confer;
> A perfect annal-book, in Elzevir.
> Whate'er of glory life's first sheets presage,
> Whate'er the splendour of the title-page,
> Leaf after leaf, though learned lore ensues;
> Close as thy types and various as thy news;
> Yet, George, we see that one lot awaits them all,
> Gigantic folios, or octavos small;
> One universal finis claims his rank,
> And every volume closes in a blank.

In the churchyard of Bury St. Edmunds, Suffolk, is a good specimen of a typographical epitaph, placed in remembrance of a noted printer, who died in the year 1818. It reads as follows:

> Here lie the remains of L. GEDGE, Printer.
> Like a worn-out character, he has returned to the Founder,
> Hoping that he will be re-cast in a better and
> more perfect mould.

Our next example is profuse of puns, some of which are rather obscure to younger readers, owing to the disuse of the old wooden press. It is the epitaph of a Scotch printer:—

> Sacred to the memory of
> ADAM WILLIAMSON,
> Pressman-printer, in Edinburgh,
> Who died Oct. 3, 1832,
> Aged 72 years.

All my stays are loosed ;
My cap is thrown off ; my head is worn out ;
My box is broken ;
My spindle and bar have lost their power ;
My till is laid aside ;
Both legs of my crane are turned out of their path ;
My platen can make no impression ;
My winter hath no spring ;
My rounce will neither roll out nor in ;
Stone, coffin, and carriage have all failed ;
The hinges of my tympan and frisket are immovable;
My long and short ribs are rusted ;
My cheeks are much worm-eaten and mouldering
away :
My press is totally down :
The volume of my life is finished,
Not without many errors ;
Most of them have arisen from bad composition, and
are to be attributed more to the chase than the
press ;
There are also a great number of my own :
Misses, scuffs, blotches, blurs, and bad register ;
But the true and faithful Superintendent has under-
taken to correct the whole.
When the machine is again set up
(incapable of decay),
A new and perfect edition of my life will appear,
Elegantly bound for duration, and every way fitted
for the grand Library of the Great Author.

The next specimen is less satisfactory, because devoid of the hope that should encircle the death of the Christian. It is the epitaph which Baskerville, the celebrated Birmingham printer and type founder, directed to be placed upon a tomb of masonry in the shape of a cone, and erected over his remains :—

> Stranger
> Beneath this cone, in unconsecrated ground,
> A friend to the liberties of mankind
> Directed his body to be inurned.
> May the example contribute to emancipate thy mind
> from the idle fears of superstition, and the
> wicked arts of priestcraft.

It is recorded that " The tomb has long since been overturned, and even the remains of the man himself desecrated and dispersed till the final day of resurrection, when the atheism which in his later years he professed, will receive assuredly so complete and overwhelming a refutation."

In 1599 died Christopher Barker, one of the most celebrated of the sixteenth century typographers, printer to Queen Elizabeth—to whom, in fact, the present patent, held by Eyre and Spottiswode, can be traced back in unbroken succession.

> Here Barker lies, once printer to the Crown,
> Whose works of art acquired a vast renown.
> Time saw his worth, and spread around his fame,
> That future printers might imprint the same.
> But when his strength could work the press no more
> And his last sheets were folded into store,
> Pure faith, with hope (the greatest treasure given),
> Opened their gates, and bade him pass to heaven.

We shall bring to a close our examples of typographical epitaphs with the following, copied from the graveyard of St. Michael's, Coventry, on a worthy printer who was engaged over sixty years as a compositor on the *Coventry Mercury* :—

Here
lies inter'd
the mortal remains
of
JOHN HULM,
Printer,
who, like an old, worn-out type,
battered by frequent use,
reposes in the grave.
But not without a hope that at some future time
he might be cast in the mould of righteousness,
And safely locked-up
in the chase of immortality.
He was distributed from the board of life
on the 9th day of Sept., 1827,
Aged 75.
Regretted by his employers,
and respected by his fellow artists.

EPITAPHS ON SPORTSMEN.

THE stirring lives of sportsmen have suggested spirited lines for their tombstones, as will be seen from the examples we bring under the notice of our readers.

The first epitaph is from Morville churchyard, near Bridgnorth, on John Charlton, Esq., who was for many years Master of the Wheatland Foxhounds, and died January 20th, 1843, aged 63 years; regretted by all who knew him :—

> Of this world's pleasure I have had my share,
> And few the sorrows I was doomed to bear.
> How oft have I enjoy'd the noble chase
> Of hounds and foxes striving for the race!
> But hark! the knell of death calls me away,
> So sportsmen, all, farewell! I must obey.

Our next is written on Mills, the huntsman :—
> Here lies John Mills, who over the hills
> Pursued the hounds with hallo:
> The leap though high, from earth to sky,
> The huntsman we must follow.

A short, rough, but pregnant epitaph is placed over the remains of Robert Hackett, a keeper of Hardwick Park, who died in 1703, and was buried in Ault Hucknall churchyard :—

>Long had he chased
>The Red and Fallow Deer,
>But Death's cold dart
>At last has fix'd him here.

George Dixon, a noted foxhunter, is buried in Luton churchyard, and on his gravestone the following appears :—

>Stop, passenger, and thy attention fix on,
>That true-born, honest, fox-hunter, GEORGE DIXON,
>Who, after eighty years' unwearied chase,
>Now rests his bones within this hallow'd place.
>A gentle tribute of applause bestow,
>And give him, as you pass, one *tally-ho !*
>Early to cover, brisk he rode each morn,
>In hopes the *brush* his temple might adorn ;
>The view is now no more, the chase is past,
>And to an earth, poor GEORGE is run at last.

On a stone in the graveyard of Mottram the following inscription appears :—

>In the memory of GEORGE NEWTON,
>of Stalybridge,
>who died August 7th, 1871,
>in the 94th year of his age.

>Though he liv'd long, the old man has gone at last,
>No more he'll hear the huntsman's stirring blast ;
>Though fleet as Reynard in his youthful prime,
>At last he's yielded to the hand of Time.

EPITAPHS ON SPORTSMEN. 23

> Blithe as a lark, dress'd in his coat of green,
> With hounds and horn the old man was seen.
> But ah ! Death came, worn out and full of years,
> He died in peace, mourn'd by his offsprings' tears.

"Let us run with patience the race that is set before us."

In the churchyard of Ecclesfield, may be read the following epitaph :—

> In memory of THOMAS RIDGE,
> the Ecclesfield huntsman,
> who died 13th day of January, 1871,
> Aged 77 years.
>
> Though fond of sport, devoted of the chase,
> And with his fellow-hunters first in place,
> He always kept the Lord's appointed day,
> Never from church or Sunday-school away.
> And now his body rests beneath the sod,
> His soul relying in the love of God.

Of the many epitaphs on sportsmen to be seen in Nottinghamshire, we cull a few of the choicest. Our first is a literal copy from a weather-worn stone in Eakring churchyard, placed to the memory of Henry Cartwright, senior keeper to his Grace the Duke of Kingston for fifty-five years, who died February 13th, 1773, aged eighty years, ten months, and three weeks :—

> My gun discharged, my ball is gone
> My powder's spent, my work is done,
> those panting deer I have left behind,
> May now have time to Gain their wind,
> Who I have oft times Chass'd them ore
> the burial Plains, but now no more.

We next present particulars of a celebrated deer-stealer. According to a notice furnished in the "Nottingham Date Book," the deeds of Tom Booth were for many years after his death a never-failing subject of conversational interest in Nottingham. It is stated that no modern deer-stealer was anything like so popular. Thorsby relates one exploit as follows: "In Nottingham Park, at one time, was a favourite fine deer, a chief ranger, on which Tom and his wily companions had often cast their eyes; but how to deceive the keeper while they killed it was a task of difficulty. The night, however, in which they accomplished their purpose—whether by any settled plan or not is not known—they found the keeper at watch, as usual, in a certain place in the park. One of them, therefore, went in an opposite direction in the park, and fired his gun to make the keeper believe he had shot a deer; upon which away goes the keeper, in haste, to the spot, which was at a very considerable distance from the place where the favourite deer was, and near which Tom Booth was skulking. Tom, waiting a proper time, when he thought the keeper at a sufficient distance for accomplishing his purpose, fired and killed the deer, and dragged it through the river Leen undiscovered." Booth was a stout man, and by trade a whitesmith. The stone marking the place of his interment is still in good preservation, and stands in St. Nicholas' burial-ground, against the southern wall of the church. It bears the following inscription:—

> Here lies a marksman, who with art and skill,
> When young and strong, fat bucks and does did kill.
> Now conquered by grim Death (go, reader, tell it!)
> He's now took leave of powder, gun, and pellet.
> A fatal dart, which in the dark did fly,
> Has laid him down, among the dead to lie.
> If any want to know the poor slave's name,
> 'Tis old Tom Booth,—ne'er ask from whence he came.

Old Tom was so highly pleased with the epitaph, which was written before his death, that he had it engraved on the stone some months before its services were required. In addition to the epitaph itself, the head-stone was made to include Booth's name, &c., and also that of his wife, blank places being left in each case for the age and time of death. Booth's compartment of the stone was in due course properly filled up; but the widow, disliking the exhibition of her name on a tombstone while living, resolved that such stone should never indicate her resting place when dead; she accordingly left an injunction that her body be interred elsewhere, and the inscription is incomplete to this day.

Some time before Amos Street, a celebrated Yorkshire huntsman died, a stone was obtained, and on it engraved the following lines:—

> This is to the memory of Old Amos,
> Who was when alive for hunting famous;

> But now his chases are all o'er,
> And here he's earth'd, of years four score.
> Upon this tomb he's often sat
> And tried to read his epitaph ;
> And thou who dost so at this moment
> Shall ere long like him be dormant.

Poor " Old Amos " passed away on October 3rd, 1777, and was buried in Birstal churchyard. The foregoing inscription may still be read.

The Rev. R. H. Whitworth tells us: "There is an old monument in the south aisle of Blidworth Church, to the memory of Thomas Leake, Esq., who was killed at Blidworth Rocking in A.D. 1598. He may be regarded as the last of the race who sat in Robin Hood's seat, if those restless Forest Chiefs, typified under that name, can be supposed ever to have sat at all. Leake held office under the Crown, but was as wild a freebooter as ever drew bow. His character is portrayed in his epitaph—

    HERE RESTS T. LEAKE WHOSE VERTUES WEERE SO KNOWNE
    IN ALL THESE PARTS THAT THIS ENGRAVED STONE
    NEEDS NAVGHT RELATE BVT HIS VNTIMELY END
    WHICH WAS IN SINGLE FIGHT: WYLST YOUTH DID LEND
    HIS AYDE TO VALOR, HEE WTH EASE OREPAST
    MANY SLYGHT DANGERS, GREATER THEN THIS LAST
    BVT WILLFVLLE FATE IN THESE THINGS GOVERNS ALL
    HEE TOWLD OVT THREESCORE YEARS BEFORE HIS FALL
    MOST OF WCH TYME HE WASTED IN THIS WOOD
    MVCH OF HIS WEALTH AND LAST OF ALL HIS BLOOD

The border of this monument is rudely panelled, each panel having some forest hunting subject in relief. There are hounds getting scent, and a hound pursuing an antlered stag; a hunting horn, ribboned; plunging and flaying knives, a cross-bow, a forest-bow, two arrows, and two hunters' belts with arrows inserted. This is his register—

<blockquote>
Thomas Leake, esquire, buried the
4th February, 1598.
</blockquote>

There is a captivating bit of romance connected with Leake's death, which occurred at Archer's Water. Although somewhat 'provectus in ætate,' he had won the affections of the landlady's daughter, much to the annoyance of the mother. Archer's Water was on the old driftroad by Blidworth, from Edinburgh to London, that by which Jeannie Deans travelled, and over which Dick Turpin rode. Hundreds of thousands of Scotch cattle went by this way to town, and there was a difficulty connected with a few of them in which Leake was concerned, and a price being set upon his head, his mother-in-law, that was to be, betrayed him to two young soldiers anxious to secure the reward, one of whom was, in the mother's eyes, the more favoured lover. Tom was always attended by two magnificent dogs and went well armed. Thrown off his guard he left his dogs in an outhouse, and entering the inn laid aside his weapons, when he was set upon and overpowered, and like many better men before him, slain.

The name of a Captain Salmond of the now extinct parish or manor of Salterford is connected with this transaction. The date of the combat is 2nd February, being the festival of the Presentation of Christ in the Temple, with which the highly interesting and historical observance of Blidworth *Rocking* is connected. Within the memory of living men, a baby decked with such flowers as the season afforded, was placed in a cradle and carried about from house to house by an old man, who received a present on the occasion. As the church is dedicated to St. Mary in connection with the Purification, the 2nd of February being the Feast Day, this is probably an interesting reminiscence of some old species of Miracle Play, or observance connected with the foundation. Anciently people from all neighbouring counties used to attend this season. Forest games were played, and amid the attendant licence and confusion, Leake came to his last grief. Not only in the church does this Ranger of the Blidworth Wood, for this was his office, possess a memorial. A large cross was erected, now standing at Fountain Dale, thus inscribed :—

Hoc crucis fragmen
Traditum a sylvicolis monumentum
Loci ubi in singulari certamine
Gladiator ille insignis
Tho. Leake
Mori occubuit
Anno MDCVIII.

> Ab antiqua sede remotum
> H. P. C.
> Joannes Downall
> Prid. Non Sext. MDCCCXXXVI.

What became of the daughter tradition sayeth not. Doubtless she died, as Tom Leake's intended bride ought, of grief, and was buried under some grand old oak in Blidworth Forest."

Let us direct attention to another class of sportsmen. At Bunney, a monument is erected to Sir Thomas Parkyns, the well-known wrestler. It bears four lines in Latin, which have been translated thus:—

> At length he falls, the long contest's o'er,
> And Time has thrown whom none e'er threw before ;
> Yet boast not (Time) thy victory, for he
> At last shall rise again and conquer thee.

The next is copied from a stone in St. Michael's churchyard, Coventry, on a famous fencing-master:—

> To the memory of Mr. John Parkes,
> A native of this City
> He was a man of mild disposition,
> A Gladiator by profession ;
> Who after having fought 350 battles,
> In the principal parts of Europe,
> With honour and applause,
> At length quitted the stage, sheathed his sword,
> And with Christian resignation,
> Submitted to the Grand Victor
> In the 52nd year of his age
> Anno Domini 1733.

An old stone bearing the foregoing inscription was replaced by a new one some years ago at the expense of the late S. Carter, Esq., formerly member of parliament for Coventry. In the pages of the *Spectator* honourable mention is made of John Parkes.

In the churchyard of Hanslope, is buried Sandy M'Kay, the Scottish giant, who was killed in a prize-fight with Simon Byrne. A headstone bears the following inscription:—

> Sacred to the memory of
> ALEX. M'KAY,
> (Late of Glasgow),
> Who died 3rd June, 1834,
> Aged 26 years.
> Strong and athletic was my frame;
> Far from my native home I came,
> And manly fought with Simon Byrne;
> Alas! but lived not to return.
> Reader, take warning of my fate,
> Lest you should rue your case too late:
> If you ever have fought before,
> Determine now to fight no more.

We are informed that Byrne was killed shortly afterwards, whilst engaged in fighting.

From the prize-ring let us turn to the more satisfactory amusement of cricket. In Highgate cemetery, Lillywhite, the celebrated cricketer, is buried, and over his remains is placed a monument with the significant emblem of a wicket being upset with a ball.

The following lines are said to be copied from the tombstone in a cemetery near Salisbury:—

> I bowl'd, I struck, I caught, I stopp'd,
> Sure life's a game of cricket ;
> I block'd with care, with caution popp'd,
> Yet Death has hit my wicket.

The Tennis Ball is introduced in an epitaph placed in St. Michael's Church, Coventry. It reads thus:—

" Here lyes the Body of Captain Gervase Scrope, of the Family of Scropes, of Bolton, in the County of York, who departed this life the 26th day of August, Anno Domini, 1705."

AN EPITAPH WRITTEN BY HIMSELF IN THE AGONY AND DOLOROUS PAINES OF THE GOUT, AND DYED SOON AFTER.

> Here lyes an Old Toss'd Tennis Ball,
> Was Racketted from Spring to Fall
> With so much heat, and so much hast,
> Time's arm (for shame) grew tyr'd at last,
> Four Kings in Camps he truly seru'd,
> And from his Loyalty ne'r sweru'd.
> Father ruin'd, the Son slighted,
> And from the Crown ne'r requited.
> Loss of Estate, Relations, Blood,
> Was too well Known, but did no good,
> With long Campaigns and paines of th' Govt,
> He cou'd no longer hold it out :
> Always a restless life he led,
> Never at quiet till quite dead,
> He marry'd in his latter dayes,
> One who exceeds the com'on praise,

> But wanting breath still to make Known
> Her true Affection and his Own,
> Death kindly came, all wants supply'd
> By giuing Rest which life deny'd.

We conclude this class of epitaphs with a couple of piscatorial examples. The first is from the churchyard of Hythe :—

> His net old fisher George long drew,
>   Shoals upon shoals he caught,
> 'Till Death came hauling for his due,
>   And made poor George his draught.
> Death fishes on through various shapes,
>   In vain it is to fret ;
> Nor fish nor fisherman escapes
>   Death's all-enclosing net.

In the churchyard of Great Yarmouth, under date of 1769, an epitaph runs thus :—

> Here lies doomed,
> In this vault so dark,
> A soldier weaver, *angler*, and clerk ;
> Death snatched him hence, and from him took
> His gun, his shuttle, fish-rod, and hook.
> He could not weave, nor fish, nor fight, so then
> He left the world, and faintly cried—Amen.

EPITAPHS ON TRADESMEN.

MANY interesting epitaphs are placed to the memory of tradesmen. Often they are not of an elevating character, nor highly poetical, but they display the whims and oddities of men. We will first present a few relating to the watch and clock-making trade. The first specimen is from Lydford churchyard, on the borders of Dartmoor :—

>Here lies, in horizontal position,
>the outside case of
>GEORGE ROUTLEIGH, Watchmaker ;
>Whose abilities in that line were an honour
>to his profession.
>Integrity was the Mainspring, and prudence the
>Regulator,
>of all the actions of his life.
>Humane, generous, and liberal,
>his Hand never stopped
>till he had relieved distress.
>So nicely regulated were all his motions,
>that he never went wrong,

>   except when set a-going
>   by people
>   who did not know his Key ;
>   even then he was easily
>   set right again.
>   He had the art of disposing his time so well,
>   that his hours glided away
>   in one continual round
>   of pleasure and delight,
>   until an unlucky minute put a period to
>   his existence.
>   He departed this life
>   Nov. 14, 1802,
>   aged 57 :
>   wound up,
>   in hopes of being taken in hand
>   by his Maker ;
>   and of being thoroughly cleaned, repaired,
>   and set a-going
>   in the world to come.

In the churchyard of Uttoxeter, a monument is placed to the memory of Joseph Slater, who died November 21st, 1822, aged 49 years :—

> Here lies one who strove to equal time,
> A task too hard, each power too sublime ;
> Time stopt his motion, o'erthrew his balance-wheel,
> Wore off his pivots, tho' made of hardened steel ;
> Broke all his springs, the verge of life decayed,
> And now he is as though he'd ne'er been made.
> Such frail machine till time's no more shall rust,
> And the archangel wakes our sleeping dust ;
> Then in assembled worlds in glory join,
> And sing—" The hand that made us is divine."

Our next is from Berkeley, Gloucestershire :—

> Here lyeth Thomas Peirce, whom no man taught,
> Yet he in iron, brass, and silver wrought ;
> He jacks, and clocks, and watches (with art) made
> And mended, too, when others' work did fade.
> Of Berkeley, five times Mayor this artist was,
> And yet this Mayor, this artist, was but grass.
> When his own watch was down on the last day,
> He that made watches had not made a key
> To wind it up ; but useless it must lie,
> Until he rise again no more to die.
>   Died February 25th, 1665, aged 77.

The following is from Bolsover churchyard, Derbyshire :—

> Here
> lies, in a horizontal position, the outside
> case of
> THOMAS HINDE,
> Clock and Watch-maker,
> Who departed this life, wound up in hope of
> being taken in hand by his Maker, and being
> thoroughly cleaned, repaired, and set a-going
> in the world to come,
> On the 15th of August, 1836,
> In the 19th year of his age.

Respecting the next example, our friend, Mr. Edward Walford, M.A., wrote to the *Times* as follows : " Close to the south-western corner of the parish churchyard of Hampstead there has long stood a square tomb, with a scarcely decipherable inscription, to the memory of a man of science of the last century, whose name is connected with the history of practical navigation. The tomb, having stood there for more than a century, had become somewhat dilapidated, and has lately undergone a careful restoration at the cost and under the supervision of the Company of Clockmakers, and the fact is recorded in large characters on the upper face. The tops of the upright iron railings which surround the tomb have been gilt, and the restored inscription runs as follows: 'In memory of Mr. John Harrison, late of Red Lion-square, London, inventor of the time-keeper for ascertaining the longitude at sea. He was born at Foulby, in the county of York, and was the son of a builder of that place, who brought him up to the same profession. Before he attained the age of 21, he, without any instruction, employed himself in cleaning and repairing clocks and watches, and made a few of the former, chiefly of wood. At the age of 25 he employed his whole time in chronometrical improvements. He was the inventor of the gridiron pendulum, and the method of preventing the effects of heat and cold upon time-keepers by two bars fixed together; he introduced the secondary spring, to keep them going while winding up, and was the inventor of most or all) the improvements in clocks and watches during his time. In the year 1735 his first time-keeper was sent to Lisbon, and in 1764 his then much improved fourth time-keeper having been sent to Barbadoes, the Commissioners of Longitude certified that he had determined the longitude within one-third of half a degree of a great circle, having not erred more than forty seconds in time. After sixty years' close application to the above pursuits, he departed this life on the 24th day of March, 1776, aged 83.

In an epitaph in High Wycombe churchyard, life is compared to the working of a clock. It runs thus :—

>   Of no distemper,
>   Of no blast he died,
>   But fell,
>   Like Autumn's fruit,
>   That mellows long,
>   Even wondered at
>   Because he dropt not sooner.
>   Providence seemed to wind him up
>   For fourscore years,
>   Yet ran he nine winters more ;
>   Till, like a clock,
>   Worn out with repeating time,
>   The wheels of weary life
>   At last stood still.
>   In memory of JOHN ABDIDGE, Alderman.
>   Died 1785.

We have some curious specimens of engineers' epitaphs. A good example is copied from the churchyard of Bridgeford-on-the-Hill, Notts :—

> Sacred to the Memory of JOHN WALKER, the only son of Benjamin and Ann Walker, Engineer and Pallisade Maker, died September 22nd, 1832, aged 36 years.
>   Farewell, my wife and father dear ;
>   My glass is run, my work is done,

And now my head lies quiet here.
That many an engine I've set up,
And got great praise from men,
I made them work on British ground,
And on the roaring seas ;
My engine's stopp'd, my valves are bad,
And lie so deep within ;
No engineer could there be found
To put me new ones in.
But Jesus Christ converted me
And took me up above,
I hope once more to meet once more,
And sing redeeming love.

Our next is on a railway engineer, who died in 1840, and was buried in Bromsgrove churchyard :—

My engine now is cold and still,
No water does my boiler fill ;
My coke affords its flame no more
My days of usefulness are o'er ;
My wheels deny their noted speed,
No more my guiding hand they need ;
My whistle, too, has lost its tone,
Its shrill and thrilling sounds are gone ;
My valves are now thrown open wide ;
My flanges all refuse to guide,
My clacks also, though once so strong,
Refuse to aid the busy throng :
No more I feel each urging breath ;
My steam is now condensed in death.
Life's railway o'er, each station's passed,
In death I'm stopped, and rest at last.
Farewell, dear friends, and cease to weep :
In Christ I'm safe ; in Him I sleep.

The epitaph we next give is on the driver of the coach that ran between Aylesbury and London, by the Rev. H. Bullen, Vicar of Dunton, Bucks, in whose churchyard the man was buried :—

> Parker, farewell ! thy journey now is ended,
> Death has the whip-hand, and with dust is blended ;
> Thy way-bill is examined, and I trust
> Thy last account may prove exact and just.
> When he who drives the chariot of the day,
> Where life is light, whose Word's the living way,
> Where travellers, like yourself, of every age,
> And every clime, have taken their last stage,
> The God of mercy, and the God of love,
> Show you the road to Paradise above !

Lord Byron wrote on John Adams, carrier, of Southwell, Nottinghamshire, an epitaph as follows :—

> John Adams lies here, of the parish of Southwell,
> A carrier who carried his can to his mouth well ;
> He carried so much, and he carried so fast
> He could carry no more—so was carried at last ;
> For the liquor he drank, being too much for one,
> He could not carry off—so he's now carri-on.

On Hobson, the famous University carrier, the following lines were written :—

> Here lies old Hobson : death has broke his girt,
> And here ! alas, has laid him in the dirt ;
> Or else the ways being foul, twenty to one
> He's here stuck in a slough and overthrown :
> 'Twas such a shifter, that, if truth were known,
> Death was half glad when he had got him down ;

For he had any time these ten years full,
Dodged with him betwixt Cambridge and the Bull;
And surely Death could never have prevailed,
Had not his weekly course of carriage failed.
But lately finding him so long at home,
And thinking now his journey's end was come,
And that he had ta'en up his latest inn,
In the kind office of a chamberlain
Showed him the room where he must lodge that night,
Pulled off his boots and took away the light.
If any ask for him it shall be said,
Hobson has supt and's newly gone to bed.

In Trinity churchyard, Sheffield, formerly might be seen an epitaph on a bookseller, as follows:—

In Memory of
RICHARD SMITH, who died
April 6th, 1757, aged 52.
At thirteen years I went to sea;
  To try my fortune there,
But lost my friend, which put an end
  To all my interest there.
To land I came as 'twere by chance,
At twenty then I taught to dance,
And yet unsettled in my mind,
To something else I was inclined;
At twenty-five laid dancing down,
To be a bookseller in this town,
Where I continued without strife,
Till death deprived me of my life.
Vain world, to thee I bid farewell,
To rest within this silent cell,

Till the great God shall summon all
To answer His majestic call,
Then, Lord, have mercy on us all.

The following epitaph was written on James Lackington, a celebrated bookseller, and eccentric character :—

> Good passenger, one moment stay,
> And contemplate this heap of clay ;
> 'Tis LACKINGTON that claims a pause,
> Who strove with death, but lost his cause :
> A stranger genius ne'er need be
> Than many a merry year was he.
> Some faults he had, some virtues too
> (The devil himself should have his due);
> And as dame fortune's wheel turn'd round,
> Whether at top or bottom found,
> He never once forgot his station,
> Nor e'er disown'd a poor relation ;
> In poverty he found content,
> Riches ne'er made him insolent.
> When poor, he'd rather read than eat,
> When rich books form'd his highest treat,
> His first great wish to act, with care,
> The sev'ral parts assigned him here ;
> And, as his heart to truth inclin'd,
> He studied hard the truth to find.
> Much pride he had,—'twas love of fame,
> And slighted gold, to get a name ;
> But fame herself prov'd greatest gain,
> For riches follow'd in her train.
> Much had he read, and much had thought,
> And yet, you see, he's come to nought ;

> Or out of print, as he would say,
> To be revised some future day:
> Free from errata, with addition,
> A new and a complete edition.

At Rugby, on Joseph Cave, Dr. Hawksworth, wrote:—

> Near this place lies the body of
> JOSEPH CAVE,
> Late of this parish;
> Who departed this life Nov. 18, 1747,
> Aged 79 years.

He was placed by Providence in a humble station; but industry abundantly supplied the wants of nature, and temperance blest him with content and wealth. As he was an affectionate father, he was made happy in the decline of life by the deserved eminence of his eldest son,

> EDWARD CAVE,

who, without interest, fortune, or connection, by the native force of his own genius, assisted only by a classical education, which he received at the Grammar School of this town, planned, executed, and established a literary work called

> *The Gentleman's Magazine,*

whereby he acquired an ample fortune, the whole of which devolved to his family.

> Here also lies
> The body of WILLIAM CAVE,

second son of the said JOSEPH CAVE, who died May 2, 1757, aged 62 years, and who, having survived his elder brother,

> EDWARD CAVE,

inherited from him a competent estate; and, in gratitude to his benefactor, ordered this monument to perpetuate his memory.

> He lived a patriarch in his numerous race,
> And shew'd in charity a Christian's grace:
> Whate'er a friend or parent feels he knew;
> His hand was open, and his heart was true;
> In what he gain'd and gave, he taught mankind
> A grateful always is a generous mind.
> Here rests his clay! his soul must ever rest,
> Who bless'd when living, dying must be blest.

The well-known blacksmith's epitaph, said to be written by the poet Hayley, may be found in many churchyards in this country. It formed the subject of a sermon delivered on Sunday, the 27th day of August, 1837, by the then Vicar of Crich, Derbyshire, to a large assembly. We are told that the vicar appeared much excited, and read the prayers in a hurried manner. Without leaving the desk, he proceeded to address his flock for the last time; and the following is the substance thereof: "To-morrow, my friends, this living will be vacant, and if any one of you is desirous of becoming my successor he has now an opportunity. Let him use his influence, and who can tell but he may be honoured with the title of Vicar of Crich. As this is my last address, I shall only say, had I been a blacksmith, or a son of Vulcan, the following lines might not have been inappropriate:—

> My sledge and hammer lie reclined,
> My bellows, too, have lost their wind;
> My fire's extinct, my forge decayed,
> And in the dust my vice is laid.

> My coal is spent, my iron's gone,
> My nails are drove, my work is done;
> My fire-dried corpse lies here at rest,
> And, smoke-like, soars up to be bless'd.

If you expect anything more, you are deceived; for I shall only say, Friends, farewell, farewell!" The effect of this address was too visible to pass unnoticed. Some appeared as if awakened from a fearful dream, and gazed at each other in silent astonishment; others for whom it was too powerful for their risible nerves to resist, burst into boisterous laughter, while one and all slowly retired from the scene, to exercise their future cogitations on the farewell discourse of their late pastor.

From Silkstone churchyard we have the following on a Potter and his wife :—

In memory of John Taylor, of Silkstone, potter, who departed this life, July 14th, Anno Domini 1815, aged 72 years.

Also Hannah, his wife, who departed this life, August 13th, 1815, aged 68 years.

> Out of the clay they got their daily bread,
> Of clay were also made.
> Returned to clay they now lie dead,
> Where all that's left must shortly go.
> To live without him his wife she tried,
> Found the task hard, fell sick, and died.
> And now in peace their bodies lay,
> Until the dead be called away,
> And moulded into spiritual clay.

On a poor woman who kept an earthenware shop at Chester, the following epitaph was composed:—

> Beneath this stone lies CATHERINE GRAY,
> Changed to a lifeless lump of clay;
> By earth and clay she got her pelf,
> And now she's turned to earth herself.
> Ye weeping friends, let me advise,
> Abate your tears and dry your eyes;
> For what avails a flood of tears?
> Who knows but in a course of years,
> In some tall pitcher or brown pan,
> She in her shop may be again.

Our next is from the churchyard of Aliscombe, Devonshire:—

Here lies the remains of JAMES PADY, brickmaker, late of this parish, in hopes that his clay will be remoulded in a workmanlike manner, far superior to his former perishable materials.

> Keep death and judgment always in your eye,
> Or else the devil off with you will fly,
> And in his kiln with brimstone ever fry:
> If you neglect the narrow road to seek,
> Christ will reject you, like a half-burnt brick!

In the old churchyard of Bullingham, on the gravestone of a builder, the following lines appear:—

> This humble stone is o'er a builder's bed,
> Tho' raised on high by fame, low lies his head.
> His rule and compass are now locked up in store.
> Others may build, but he will build no more.
> His house of clay so frail, could hold no longer—
> May he in heaven be tenant of a stronger!

In Colton churchyard, Staffordshire, is a mason's tombstone decorated with carving of square and compass, in relief, and bearing the following characteristic inscription: —

> Sacred to the memory of
> JAMES HEYWOOD,
> Who died May 4th, 1804, in the 55th
> year of his age.
> The corner-stone I often times have dress'd ;
> In Christ, the corner-stone, I now find rest.
> Though by the Builder he rejected were,
> He is my God, my Rock, I build on here.

In the churchyard of Longnor the following quaint epitaph is placed over the remains of a carpenter :—

> IN
> Memory of SAMUEL
> BAGSHAW late of Har-
> ding-booth who depar-
> ted this life June the
> 5th 1787 aged 71 years.

Beneath lie mouldering into Dust
A Carpenter's Remains.
A man laborious, honest, just : his Character sustains.
In seventy-one revolving Years
He sow'd no Seeds of Strife ;
With Ax and Saw, Line, Rule and Square, employed his careful life.
But Death who view'd his peaceful Lot
His Tree of Life assail'd
His Grave was made upon this spot, and his last Branch he nail'd.

Our next is from Hessle, near Hull, where over the remains of George Prissick, plumber and glazier, is the following epitaph :—

> Adieu, my friend, my thread of life is spun ;
> The diamond will not cut, the solder will not run ;
> My body's turned to ashes, my grief and troubles past,
> I've left no one to worldly care—and I shall rise at last.

On a dyer, from the church of St. Nicholas, Yarmouth, we have as follows :—

> Here lies a man who first did dye,
> When he was twenty four,
> And yet he lived to reach the age,
> Of hoary hairs, fourscore.
> But now he's gone, and certain 'tis
> He'll not dye any more.

In Sleaford churchyard, on Henry Fox, a weaver, the following lines are inscribed :—

> Of tender thread this mortal web is made,
> The woof and warp and colours early fade ;
> When power divine awakes the sleeping dust,
> He gives immortal garments to the just.

Our next epitaph from Weston, is placed over the remains of a useful member of society in his time :—

> Here lies entomb'd within this vault so dark,
> A tailor, cloth-drawer, soldier, and parish clerk ;
> Death snatch'd him hence, and also from him took
> His needle, thimble, sword, and prayer-book.
> He could not work, nor fight,—what then ?
> He left the world, and faintly cried, " Amen !"

On an Oxford bellows-maker, the following lines were written :—

> Here lyeth John Cruker, a maker of bellowes,
> His craftes-master and King of good fellowes ;
> Yet when he came to the hour of his death,
> He that made bellowes, could not make breath.

The next epitaph, on Joseph Blakett, poet and shoe-maker of Seaham, is said to be from Byron's pen :—

> Stranger ! behold interr'd together
> The souls of learning and of leather.
> Poor Joe is gone, but left his awl—
> You'll find his relics in a stall.
> His work was neat, and often found
> Well-stitched and with morocco bound.
> Tread lightly—where the bard is laid
> We cannot mend the shoe he made ;
> Yet he is happy in his hole,
> With verse immortal as his sole.
> But still to business he held fast,
> And stuck to Phœbus to the last.
> Then who shall say so good a fellow
> Was only leather and prunella ?
> For character—he did not lack it,
> And if he did—'twere shame to Black it !

The following lines are on a cobbler :—

> Death at a cobbler's door oft made a stand,
> But always found him on the mending hand ;
> At length Death came, in very dirty weather,
> And ripp'd the soul from off the upper leather :
> The cobbler lost his all,—Death gave his last,
> And buried in oblivion all the past.

Respecting Robert Gray, a correspondent writes: He was a native of Taunton, and at an early age he lost his parents, and went to London to seek his fortune. Here, as an errand boy, he behaved so well, that his master took him apprentice, and afterwards set him up in business, by which he made a large fortune. In his old age he retired from trade and returned to Taunton, where he founded a hospital. On his monument is the following inscription:—

> Taunton bore him; London bred him;
> Piety train'd him; Virtue led him;
> Earth enrich'd him; Heaven possess'd him;
> Taunton bless'd him; London bless'd him:
> This thankful town, that mindful city,
> Share his piety and pity,
> What he gave, and how he gave it,
> Ask the poor, and you shall have it.
> Gentle reader, may Heaven strike
> Thy tender heart to do the like;
> And now thy eyes have read his story,
> Give him the praise, and God the glory.

He died at the age of 65 years, in 1635.

In Rotherham churchyard the following is inscribed on a miller:—

> In memory of
> EDWARD SWAIR,
> who departed this life, June 16, 1781.
>
> Here lies a man which Farmers lov'd
> Who always to them constant proved;
> Dealt with freedom, Just and Fair—
> An honest miller all declare.

On a Bristol baker we have the following:—

Here lies THO. TURAR, and MARY, his wife. He was twice Master of the Company of Bakers, and twice Churchwarden of this parish. He died March 6, 1654. She died May 8th, 1643.

> Like to the baker's oven is the grave,
> Wherein the bodyes of the faithful have
> A setting in, and where they do remain
> In hopes to rise, and to be drawn again;
> Blessed are they who in the Lord are dead,
> Though set like dough, they shall be drawn like bread.

Here are some witty lines on a carpenter named John Spong, who died 1739, and is buried in Ockham churchyard:—

> Who many a sturdy oak has laid along,
> Fell'd by Death's surer hatchet, here lies JOHN SPONG.
> Post oft he made, yet ne'er a place could get
> And lived by railing, tho' he was no wit.
> Old saws he had, although no antiquarian;
> And stiles corrected, yet was no grammarian.
> Long lived he Ockham's favourite architect,
> And lasting as his fame a tomb t' erect,
> In vain we seek an artist such as he,
> Whose pales and piles were for eternity.

On the tomb of an auctioneer in the churchyard at Corby, in the county of Lincoln, we have found:—

> Beneath this stone, facetious wight
> Lies all that's left of Poor Joe Wright;
> Few heads with knowledge more informed,
> Few hearts with friendship better warmed;

With ready wit and humour broad,
He pleased the peasant, squire, and lord ;
Until grim death, with visage queer,
Assumed Joe's trade of Auctioneer,
Made him the Lot to *practise* on,
With "going, going," and anon
He knocked him down to "Poor Joe's gone!"

In Wimbledon churchyard is the grave of John Martin, a natural son of Don John Emanuel, King of Portugal. He was sent to this country about the year 1712, to be out of the way of his friends, and after several changes of circumstances, ultimately became a gardener. It will be seen from the following epitaph that he won the esteem of his employers :—

To the memory of John Martin, gardener, a native of Portugal, who cultivated here, with industry and success, the same ground under three masters, forty years.

> Though skilful and experienced,
> He was modest and unassuming ;
> And tho' faithful to his masters,
> And with reason esteemed,
> He was kind to his fellow-servants,
> And was therefore beloved.
> His family and neighbours lamented his death,
> As he was a careful husband, a tender father,
>   and an honest man.

This character of him is given to posterity by his last master, willingly because deservedly, as a lasting testimony of his great regard for so good a servant.

He died March 30th, 1760. Aged 66 years.

> For public service grateful nations raise
> Proud structures, which excite to deeds of praise;
> While private services, in corners thrown,
> Howe'er deserving, never gain a stone.
>
> But are not lilies, which the valleys hide,
> Perfect as cedars, tho' the valley's pride?
> Let, then, the violets their fragrance breathe,
> And pines their ever-verdant branches wreathe
>
> Around his grave, who from their tender birth
> Upreared both dwarf and giant sons of earth,
> And tho' himself exotic, lived to see
> Trees of his raising droop as well as he.
>
> Those were his care, while his own bending age,
> His master propp'd and screened from winter's rage,
> Till down he gently fell, then with a tear
> He bade his sorrowing sons transport him here.
>
> But tho' in weakness planted, as his fruit
> Always bespoke the goodness of his root,
> The spirit quickening, he in power shall rise
> With leaf unfading under happier skies.

The next is on the Tradescants, famous gardeners and botanists at Lambeth. In 1657 Mr. Tradescant, Junr., presented to the Ashmolean Museum, Oxford, a remarkable cabinet of curiosities:—

> Know, stranger, ere thou pass, beneath this stone
> Lye John Tradescant, grandsire, father, son;
> The last died in his spring; the other two
> Liv'd till they had travell'd art and nature through;
> As by their choice collections may appear,
> Of what is rare, in land, in sea, in air;

> Whilst they (as Homer's Iliad in a nut)
> A world of wonders in one closet shut;
> These famous antiquarians, that had been
> Both gard'ners to the ROSE AND LILY QUEEN,
> Transplanted now themselves, sleep here; and when
> Angels shall with trumpets waken men,
> And fire shall purge the world, these hence shall rise,
> And change this garden for a paradise.

We have here an epitaph on a grocer, culled from the Rev. C. W. Bardsley's "Memorials of St. Anne's Church," Manchester. In a note about the name of Howard, the author says: " Poor John Howard's friends gave him an unfortunate epitaph—one, too, that reflected unkindly upon his wife. It may still be seen in the churchyard.—Here lyeth the body of John Howard, who died Jan. 2, 1800, aged 84 years; fifty years a respectable grocer, and an honest man. As it is further stated that his wife died in 1749, fifty years before, it would seem that her husband's honesty dated from the day of her decease. Mrs. Malaprop herself, in her happiest moments, could not have beaten this inscription."

BACCHANALIAN EPITAPHS.

SOME singular epitaphs are to be found over the remains of men who either manufactured, dispensed, or loved the social glass. In the churchyard of Newhaven, the Sussex, following may be seen on the grave of a brewer:

To the Memory of
THOMAS TIPPER who
departed this life May the 14th
1785 Aged 54 Years.

READER, with kind regard this GRAVE survey
Nor heedless pass where TIPPER's ashes lay,
Honest he was, ingenuous, blunt, and kind;
And dared do, what few dare do, speak his mind,
PHILOSOPHY and HISTORY well he knew,
Was versed in PHYSICK and in Surgery too,
The best old STINGO he both brewed and sold,
Nor did one knavish act to get his Gold.
He played through Life a varied comic part,
And knew immortal HUDIBRAS by heart.
READER, in real truth, such was the Man,
Be better, wiser, laugh more if you can.

The next, on John Scott, a Liverpool brewer, is rather rich in puns:—

> Poor JOHN SCOTT lies buried here;
> Although he was both hale and stout,
> Death stretched him on the bitter bier.
> In another world he hops about.

On a Butler in Ollerton church-yard is the following curious epitaph:—

> Beneath the droppings of this spout,
> Here lies the body once so stout,
>   Of Francis Thompson.
> A soul this carcase once possess'd,
> Which of its virtues was caress'd,
> By all who knew the owner best.
> The Rufford records can declare,
> His actions, who for seventy year,
> Both drew and drank its potent beer;
> Fame mentions not in all that time,
> In this great Butler the least crime,
>   To stain his reputation.
> To envy's self we now appeal,
> If aught of fault she can reveal,
>   To make her declaration.
> Here rest good shade, nor hell nor vermin fear,
> Thy virtues guard thy soul, thy body good strong beer.
>   He died July 6th, 1739.

We will next give a few epitaphs on publicans. Our first is from Pannal churchyard; it is on JOSEPH THACKEREY, who died on the 26th of November, 1791:—

In the year of our Lord 1740
I came to the Crown ;
In 1791 they laid me down.

The following is from the graveyard of Upton-on-Severn, and placed to the memory of a publican. The lines, it will be seen, are a dexterous weaving of the spiritual with the temporal:—

Beneath this stone, in hope of Zion,
Doth lie the landlord of the " Lion,"
His son keeps on the business still,
Resign'd unto the Heavenly will.

In 1789 passed away the landlady of the " Pig and Whistle," Greenwich, and the following lines were inscribed to her memory :—

Assign'd by Providence to rule a tap,
My days pass'd gibly, till an awkward rap,
Some way, like bankruptcy, impell'd me down.
But up I got again and shook my gown
In gamesome gambols, quite as brisk as ever,
Blithe as the lark and gay as sunny weather ;
Composed with creditors, at five in pound,
And frolick'd on till laid beneath this ground.
The debt of Nature must, you know, be paid,
No trust from her—God grant *extent in aid*.

On an inn-keeper in Stockbridge, the next may be seen :—

In memory of
JOHN BUCKETT,
Many years landlord of the King's
Head Inn, in this Borough,
Who departed this life Nov. 2, 1802.
Aged 67 years.

BACCHANALIAN EPITAHPS. 57

And is, alas! poor Buckett gone?
Farewell, convivial, honest John.
Oft at the well, by fatal stroke,
Buckets, like pitchers, must be broke.
In this same motley shifting scene,
How various have thy fortunes been!
Now lifted high—now sinking low.
To-day thy brim would overflow,
Thy bounty then would all supply,
To fill and drink, and leave thee dry;
To-morrow sunk as in a well,
Content, unseen, with truth to dwell:
But high or low, or wet or dry,
No rotten stave could malice spy.
Then rise, immortal Buckett, rise,
And claim thy station in the skies;
'Twixt Amphora and Pisces shine,
Still guarding Stockbridge with thy sign.

From the "Sportive Wit: the Muses' Merriment," issued in 1656, we extract the following lines on John Taylor, "the Water Poet," who was a native of Gloucester, and died in Phœnix Alley, London, in the 75th year of his age. You may find him, if the worms have not devoured him, in Covent Garden Churchyard:—

Here lies John Taylor, without rime or reason,
For death struck his muse in so cold a season,
That Jack lost the use of his scullers to row:
The chill pate rascal would not let his boat go.
Alas, poor Jack Taylor! this 'tis to drink ale
With nutmegs and ginger, with a taste though stale,

It drencht thee in rimes. Hadst thou been of the pack
With Draiton and Johnson to quaff off thy sack,
They'd infus'd thee a genius should ne'er expire,
And have thaw'd thy muse with elemental fire.
Yet still, for the honour of thy sprightly wit,
Since some of thy fancies so handsomely hit,
The nymphs of the rivers for thy relation
Sirnamed thee the *water-poet* of the nation.
Who can write more of thee let him do't for me.
A —— take all rimers, Jack Taylor, but thee.
    Weep not, reader, if thou canst chuse,
    Over the stone of so merry a muse.

Robert Burns wrote the following epitaph on John Dove, innkeeper, Mauchline :—

    Here lies Johnny Pigeon :
    What was his religion ?
        Whae'er desires to ken,
    To some other warl'
    Maun follow the carl,
        For here Johnny had none !
    Strong ale was ablution—
    Small beer persecution,
        A dram was *memento mori* ;
    But a full flowing bowl
    Was the saving of his soul,
        And port was celestial glory.

We extract, from a collection of epitaphs, the following on a publican :—

    A jolly landlord once was I,
    And kept the Old King's Head hard by,

> Sold mead and gin, cider and beer,
> And eke all other kinds of cheer,
> Till Death my license took away,
> And put me in this house of clay :
> A house at which you all must call,
> Sooner or later, great or small.

It is stated in Mr. J. Potter Briscoe's entertaining volume, " Nottinghamshire Facts and Fictions," that in the churchyard of Edwalton is a gravestone to the memory of Mrs. Freland, a considerable land-owner, who died in 1741 ; but who, it would appear from the inscription, was a very free liver, for her memorial says:

> She drank good ale, strong punch and wine,
> And lived to the age of ninety-nine.

A gravestone in Darneth Churchyard, near Dartford, bears the following epitaph :—

> Oh, the liquor he did love, but never will no more,
> For what he lov'd did turn his foe :
> For on the 28th of January 1741, that fatal day,
> The Debt he owed he then did pay.

At Chatham, on a drunkard, good advice is given :—

> Weep not for him, the warmest tear that's shed
> Falls unavailing o'er the unconscious dead ;
> Take the advice these friendly lines would give,
> Live not to drink, but only drink to live.

From Tonbridge churchyard we glean the following:—

> Hail !
> This stone marks the spot
> Where a notorious sot
> Doth lie ;

>   Whether at rest or not
>   It matters not
>   To you or I.
> Oft to the " Lion " he went to fill his horn.
> Now to the "Grave" he's gone to get it warm.
>
> *Beered by public subscription by his hale and stout companions, who deeply lament his absence.*

On a gravestone in the churchyard of Eton, placed to the memory of an innkeeper, it is stated :—

> Life's an inn ; my house will shew it :
> I thought so once, but now I know it.
> Man's life is but a winter's day ;
> Some only breakfast and away ;
> Others to dinner stop, and are full fed ;
> The oldest man but sups and then to bed :
> Large is his debt who lingers out the day ;
> He who goes soonest has the least to pay.

Similar epitaphs to the foregoing may be found in many churchyards in this country. In Micklehurst churchyard, an inscription runs thus :—

> Life is an Inn, where all men bait,
> The waiter, Time, the landlord, Fate ;
> Death is the score by all men due,
> I've paid my shot—and so must you.

In the old burial ground in Castle Street, Hull, on the gravestone of a boy, a slightly different version of the rhyme appears :—

> In memory of
> John, the Son of John and
> Ann Bywater, died 25th January,
> 1815, aged 14 years.

> Life's like an Inn, where Travellers stay,
> Some only breakfast and away;
> Others to dinner stay, and are full fed;
> The oldest only sup and go to bed;
> Long is the bill who lingers out the day,
> Who goes the soonest has the least to pay.

The churchyard of Melton Mowbray furnishes another rendering of the lines:—

> This world's an Inn, and I her guest:
> I've eat and drank and took my rest
> With her awhile, and now I pay
> Her lavish bill and go my way.

The foregoing inscriptions, comparing life to a house, remind us of a curious inscription in Folkestone churchyard:—

> In memory of
> REBECCA ROGERS,
> who died Aug. 22, 1688,
> Aged 44 years.
>
> A house she hath, it's made of such good fashion
> The tenant ne'er shall pay for reparation,
> Nor will her landlord ever raise the rent,
> Or turn her out of doors for non-payment;
> From chimney money, too, this call is free,
> To such a house, who would not tenant be.

In "Chronicles of the Tombs," by Thomas Joseph Pettigrew, published in 1857, it is stated respecting the foregoing epitaph: "Smoke money or chimney money is now collected at Battle, in Sussex, each householder paying one penny to the Lord of the Manor. It is also levied upon the inhabitants of the New Forest, in Hants, for the right of cutting peat and turf for fuel. And from 'Audley's Companion to the Almanac,' page 76, we learn that 'anciently, even in England, Whitsun farthings, or smoke farthings, were a composition for offerings made in the Whitsun week, by every man who occupied a house with a chimney, to the cathedral of the diocese in which he lived.' The late Mr. E. B. Price has observed, in *Notes and Queries*, (Vol. ii. p. 379), that there is a church at Northampton, upon which is an inscription recording that the expense of repairing it was defrayed by a grant of chimney money for, I believe, seven years, temp. Charles II."

In the burial-ground of St. Michael's Church, London, was interred one of the waiters of the famous Boar's Head Tavern :—

Here lieth the bodye of ROBERT PRESTON, late Drawer at the Boar's Head Tavern, Great Eastcheap, who departed this Life, March 16, Anno Domini 1730, aged 27 years.

> Bacchus, to give the topeing world surprize,
> Produc'd one sober son, and here he lies.
> Tho' nurs'd among full Hogsheads, he defy'd
> The charm of wine and ev'ry vice beside.
> O Reader, if to Justice thou'rt inclined,
> Keep Honest Preston daily in thy Mind.
> He drew good wine, took care to fill his pots,

Had sundry virtues that outweighed his fauts, (*sic*)
You that on Bacchus have the like dependence,
Pray copy Bob, in measure and attendance.

The next example from Abesford, on an exciseman, is entitled to a place among Bacchanalian epitaphs :—

No supervisor's check he fears—
Now no commissioner obeys ;
He's free from cares, entreaties, tears,
And all the heavenly oil surveys.

In the churchyard of North Wingfield, Derbyshire, a gravestone bears the following inscription :—

In Memory of THOMAS, son of JOHN and MARY CLAY, who departed this life December 16th 1724, in the 40th year of his age.

What though no mournful kindred stand
 Around the solemn bier,
No parents wring the trembling hand,
 Or drop the silent tear.

No costly oak adorned with art
 My weary limbs inclose ;
No friends impart a winding-sheet
 To deck my last repose.

The cause of the foregoing curious epitaph is thus explained. Thomas Clay was a man of intemperate habits, and at the time of his death was indebted to the village innkeeper, named Adlington, to the amount of twenty pounds. The publican resolved to seize the body ; but the parents of the deceased carefully kept the door locked until the day appointed for the funeral. As soon as the door was opened, Adlington rushed into the house, seized the corpse, and placed it on a form in the open street in front of the residence of the parents of the departed. Clay's friends refused to discharge the publican's account. After the body had been exposed for several days, Adlington committed it to the ground in a *bacon chest*.

We conclude this class of epitaphs with the following from Winchester churchyard:—

In memory of
THOMAS THETCHER,
a Grenadier in the North Regiment of Hants Militia,
who died of a violent fever contracted by drinking small
beer when hot
the 12th of May, 1764, aged 26 years.
In grateful remembrance of whose universal goodwill
towards his comrades this stone is placed here at their expense, as
a small testimony of their regard and concern.

Here sleeps in peace a Hampshire Grenadier,
Who caught his death by drinking cold small beer;
Soldiers, be wise from his untimely fall,
And when ye're hot drink strong, or none at all.

This memorial, being decayed, was restored by the officers of the garrison, A.D. 1781 :—

An honest soldier never is forgot,
Whether he die by musket or by pot.

This stone was placed by the North Hants Militia, when disembodied at Winchester, on 26th April, 1802, in consequence of the original stone being destroyed.

EPITAPHS ON SOLDIERS AND SAILORS.

WE give a few of the many curious epitaphs placed to the memory of soldiers and sea-faring men. Our initial epitaph is taken from Longnor churchyard, Staffordshire, and it tells the story of an extended and eventful life :—

In memory of WILLIAM BILLINGE, who was Born in a Corn Field at Fawfield head, in this Parish, in the year 1679. At the age of 23 years he enlisted into His Majesty's service under Sir George Rooke, and was at the taking of the Fortress of Gibralter in 1704. He afterwards served under the Duke of Marlborough at Ramillies, fought on the 23rd of May, 1706, where he was wounded by a musket-shot in his thigh. Afterwards returned to his native country, and with manly courage defended his sovereign's rights in the Rebellion in 1715 and 1745. He died within the space of 150 yards of where he was born, and was interred here the 30th January, 1791, aged 112 years.

> Billeted by death, I quartered here remain,
> And when the trumpet sounds I'll rise and march again.

On a Chelsea Hospital veteran, we have the following interesting epitaph :—

> Here lies WILLIAM HISELAND,
> A Veteran, if ever Soldier was,
> Who merited well a Pension,
> If long service be a merit,
> Having served upwards of the days of Man.
> Ancient, but not superannuated ;
> Engaged in a Series of Wars,
> Civil as well as Foreign,
> Yet maimed or worn out by neither.
> His complexion was Fresh and Florid ;
> His Health Hale and Hearty ;
> His memory Exact and Ready.
> In Stature
> He exceeded the Military Size ;
> In Strength
> He surpassed the Prime of Youth ;
> And
> What rendered his age still more Patriarchal,
> When above a Hundred Years old
> He took unto him a Wife !
> Read ! fellow Soldiers, and reflect
> That there is a Spiritual Warfare,
> As well as a Warfare *Temporal*.
> Born the 1st August, 1620,
> Died the 17th of February, 1732,
> Aged One Hundred and Twelve.

At Bremhill, Wiltshire, the following lines are placed to the memory of a soldier who reached the advanced age of 92 years :—

> A poor old soldier shall not lie unknown,
> Without a verse and this recording stone.
> 'Twas his, in youth, o'er distant lands to stray,
> Danger and death companions of his way.
> Here, in his native village, stealing age
> Closed the lone evening of his pilgrimage.
> Speak of the past—of names of high renown,
> Or brave commanders long to dust gone down,
> His look with instant animation glow'd,
> Tho' ninety winters on his head had snow'd.
> His country, while he lived, a boon supplied,
> And Faith her shield held o'er him when he died.

A correspondent states that in Battersea Church there is a handsome monument to Sir EDWARD WYNTER, a Captain in the East India Company's service in the reign of Charles II., which records that in India, where he had passed many years of his life, he was

> A rare example, and unknown to most,
> Where wealth is gain'd, and conscience is not lost;
> Nor less in martial honour was his name,
> Witness his actions of immortal fame.
> Alone, unharm'd, a tiger he opprest,
> And crush'd to death the monster of a beast.
> Thrice twenty mounted Moors he overthrew,
> Singly, on foot, some wounded, some he slew,
> Dispersed the rest,—what more could Samson do?
> True to his friends, a terror to his foes,
> Here now in peace his honour'd bones repose.

Below, in bas-relief, he is represented struggling with the tiger, both the combatants appearing in the attitude of wrestlers. He is also depicted in the performance of the yet more wonderful achievement, the discomfiture of the "thrice twenty mounted Moors," who are all flying before him.

In Yarmouth churchyard, a monumental inscription tells a painful story as follows :—

To the memory of GEORGE GRIFFITHS, of the Shropshire Militia, who died Feb 26th, 1807, in consequence of a blow received in a quarrel with his comrade.

> Time flies away as nature on its wing,
> I in a battle died (not for my King).
> Words with my brother soldier did take place,
> Which shameful is, and always brings disgrace.
> Think not the worse of him who doth remain,
> For he as well as I might have been slain.

We have also from Yarmouth the next example :—

To the memory of ISAAC SMITH, who died March 24th, 1808, and SAMUEL BODGER, who died April 2nd, 1808, both of the Cambridgeshire Militia.

> The tyrant Death did early us arrest,
> And all the magazines of life possest :
> No more the blood its circling course did run,
> But in the veins like icicles it hung ;
> No more the hearts, now void of quickening heat,
> The tuneful march of vital motion beat ;
> Stiffness did into every sinew climb,
> And a short death crept cold through every limb.

The next example is from Bury St. Edmunds:—

> WILLIAM MIDDLEDITCH,
> Late Serjeant-Major of the Grenadier Guards,
> Died Nov. 13, 1834, aged 53 years.
>
> A husband, father, comrade, friend sincere,
> A British soldier brave lies buried here.
> In Spain and Flushing, and at Waterloo,
> He fought to guard our country from the foe ;
> His comrades, Britons, who survive him, say
> He acted nobly on that glorious day.

Edward Parr died in 1811, at the age of 38 years, and was buried at North Scarle churchyard. His epitaph states:—

> A soldier once I was, as you may see,
> My King and Country claim no more from me.
> In battle I receiv'd a dreadful ball
> Severe the blow, and yet I did not fall.
> When God commands, we all must die it's true
> Farewell, dear Wife, Relations all, adieu.

A British soldier lies buried under the shadow of the fine old Minster of Beverley. He died in 1855, and his epitaph states:—

> A soldier lieth beneath the sod,
> Who many a field of battle trod :
> When glory call'd, his breast he bar'd,
> And toil and want, and danger shar'd.
> Like him through all thy duties go ;
> Waste not thy strength in useless woe,
> Heave thou no sigh and shed no tear,
> A British soldier slumbers here.

The stirring lives of many female soldiers have furnished facts for several important historical works, and rich materials for the writers of romance. We give an illustration of the stone erected by public subscription in Brighton churchyard over the remains of a notable female warrior, named Phœbe Hessel. The inscription tells the story of her long and eventful career. The closing years of her life were cheered by the liberality of George IV. During a visit to Brighton, when he was Prince Regent, he met old Phœbe, and was greatly interested in her history. He ascertained that she was supported by a few benevolent townsmen, and the kindhearted Prince questioned her respecting the amount that would be required to enable her to pass the remainder of her days in comfort. " Half-a-guinea a week" said Phœbe Hessel, " will make me as happy as a princess." That amount by order of her royal benefactor was paid to her until the day of her death. She told capital stories, had an excellent memory, and was in every respect most agreeable company. Her faculties remained unimpared to within a few hours of her death. On September 22, 1821, she was visited by a person of some literary taste, and the following particulars were obtained respecting her life. The writer states:

"I have seen to-day an extraordinary character in the person of Phœbe Hessel, a poor woman stated to be 106 years of age. It appears that she was born in March 1715, and at fifteen formed a strong attachment

> In Memory of
> **PHŒBE HESSEL,**
> who was born at Stepney, in the Year 1713.
> She served for many Years
> as a private Soldier in the 5th Regt. of foot
> in different parts of Europe
> and in the Year 1745 fought under the command
> of the DUKE of CUMBERLAND
> at the Battle of Fontenoy
> where she received a Bayonet wound in her Arm.
> Her long life which commenced in the time of
> **QUEEN ANNE**
> extended to the reign of
> **GEORGE IV.**
> by whose munificence she received comfort
> and support in her latter Years
> she died at Brighton where she had long resided
> December 12th 1821 Aged 108 Years.

A GRAVESTONE IN BRIGHTON CHURCHYARD.

to Samuel Golding, a private in the regiment called Kirk's Lambs, which was ordered to the West Indies. She determined to follow her lover, enlisted into the 5th regiment of foot, commanded by General Pearce, and embarked after him. She served there five years without discovering herself to anyone. At length they were ordered to Gibraltar. She was likewise at Montserrat, and would have been in action, but her regiment did not reach the place till the battle was decided. Her lover was wounded at Gibraltar and sent to Plymouth; she then waited on the General's lady at Gibraltar, disclosed her sex, told her story, and was immediately sent home. On her arrival, Phœbe went to Samuel Golding in the hospital, nursed him there, and when he came out, married and lived with him for twenty years; he had a pension from Chelsea. After Golding's death, she married Hessel, has had many children, and has been many years a widow. Her eldest son was a sailor with Admiral Norris: he afterwards went to the East Indies, and, if he is now alive, must be nearly seventy years of age. The rest of the family are dead. At an advanced age, she earned a scanty livelihood at Brighton by selling apples and gingerbread on the Marine Parade.

" I saw this woman to-day in her bed, to which she is confined from having lost the use of her limbs. She has even now, old and withered as she is, a characteristic countenance, and, I should judge from her present appearance, must have had a fine, though perhaps a masculine style of head when young. I have seen many a woman at the age of sixty or seventy look older than she does under the load of 108 years of human life. Her cheeks are round and seem firm, though ploughed with many a small wrinkle. Her eyes, though their sight is gone, are large and well formed. As soon as it was announced that somebody had come to see her, she broke the silence of her solitary thoughts and spoke. She began in a complaining tone, as if the remains of a strong and restless spirit were impatient of the prison of a decaying and weak body. 'Other people die, and I cannot,' she said. Upon exciting her recollection of former days, her energy seemed roused, and she spoke with emphasis. Her voice was strong for an old person; and I could easily believe her when, upon being asked if her sex was not in danger of being detected by her voice, she replied that she always had a strong and manly voice. She appeared to take a pride in having kept her secret, declaring that she told it to no man, woman, or child, during the time she was in the army; 'for you know, Sir, a drunken man and a child always tell the truth. But,' said she, 'I told my secret to the ground. I dug a hole that would hold a gallon, and whispered it there.' While I was with her the flies annoyed her extremely: she drove them away with a fan, and said they seemed to smell her out as one that was going to the grave. She showed me a wound she had received in her elbow by a bayonet. She lamented the error of her former ways, but excused it by saying, 'When you are at Rome, you must do as Rome does.' When she could not distinctly hear what was said, she raised herself in the bed and thrust her head forward with impatient energy. She said when the king saw her, he called her 'a jolly old fellow.' Though blind, she could discern a glimmering light, and I was told would frequently state the time of day by the effect of light."

The next is copied from a time-worn stone in Weem churchyard, near Aberfeldy, Perthshire :—

In memory of Captain JAMES CARMICHAEL, of Bockland's Regiment.—Died 25th Nov. 1758 :

> Where now, O Son of Mars, is Honour's aim?
> What once thou wast or wished, no more's'thy claim.
> Thy tomb, Carmichael, tells thy Honour's Roll,
> And man is born, as thee, to be forgot.
> But virtue lives to glaze thy honours o'er,
> And Heaven will smile when brittle stone's no more.

The following is inscribed on a gravestone in Fort William Cemetery :—

> Sacred
> To the Memory of
> Captain PATRICK CAMPBELL,
> Late of the 42nd Regiment,
> Who died on the xiii of December,
> MDCCCXVI.,
> Aged eighty-three years,

> A True Highlander,
> A Sincere Friend,
> And the best Deerstalker
> Of his day.

A gravestone in Barwick-in-Elmet, Yorkshire, states:—

> Here lies, retired from busy scenes,
> A first lieutenant of Marines,
> Who lately lived in gay content
> On board the brave ship "Diligent."
> Now stripp'd of all his warlike show,
> And laid in box of elm below,
> Confined in earth in narrow borders,
> He rises not till further orders.

The next is from Dartmouth Churchyard:—

> THOMAS GOLDSMITH, who died 1714.

He commanded the "Snap Dragon," as Privateer belonging to this port, in the reign of Queen Anne, in which vessel he turned pirate, and amass'd much riches.

> Men that are virtuous serve the Lord;
> And the Devil's by his friends ador'd;
> And as they merit get a place
> Amidst the bless'd or hellish race;
> Pray then, ye learned clergy show
> Where can this brute, Tom Goldsmith, go?
> Whose life was one continued evil,
> Striving to cheat God, Man, and Devil.

We find the following at Woodbridge on JOSEPH SPALDING, Master and Mariner, who departed this life

Sept. 2nd, 1796, aged 55 :—

> Embark'd in life's tempestuous sea, we steer
> 'Midst threatening billows, rocks and shoals ;
> But Christ by faith, dispels each wavering fear,
> And safe secures the anchor of our souls.

In Selby churchyard, the following is on JOHN EDMONDS, master mariner, who died 5th Aug. 1767 :—

> Tho' Boreas, with his blustering blasts
>   Has tost me to and fro
> Yet by the handiwork of God,
>   I'm here enclosed below.
> And in this silent bay I lie
>   With many of our fleet,
> Until the day that I set sail
>   My Saviour Christ to meet.

Another, on the south side of Selby churchyard :—

> The boisterous main I've travers'd o'er,
> New seas and lands explored,
> But now at last, I'm anchor'd fast,
> In peace and silence moor'd.

In the churchyard, Selby, near the north porch, in memory of WILLIAM WHITTAKER, mariner, who died 22nd Oct., 1797, we read—

> Oft time in danger have I been
>   Upon the raging main,
> But here in harbour safe at rest
>   Free from all human pain.

South-hill Church, Bedfordshire, contains a plain monument to the memory of Admiral BYNG, who was shot at Portsmouth :—

> To the perpetual disgrace of public justice,
> The Honourable JOHN BYNG, Vice Admiral of the Blue,
> fell a martyr to political persecution, March 14,
> in the year 1757 ;
> when bravery and loyalty were insufficent securities for
> the life and honour of a naval officer.

The following epitaph, inscribed on a stone in Putney Churchyard, is nearly obliterated :—

> Lieut. ALEX. DAVIDSON
> Royal Navy has Caus'd this Stone
> to be Erected to the Memory of
> HARRIOT his dearly beloved Wife
> who departed this Life Jan 24 1808
> Aged 38 Years.
>
> I have crossed this Earth's Equator Just sixteen times
> And in my Country's cause have brav'd far distant climes
> In HOWE'S TRAFALGAR and several Victories more
> Firm and unmov'd I heard the Fatal Cannons roar
> Trampling in human blood I felt not any fear
> Nor for my Slaughter'd gallant Messmates shed A tear
> But of A dear Wife by Death unhappily beguil'd
> Even the British Sailor must become A child
> Yet when from this Earth God shall my soul unfetter
> I hope we'll meet in Another World and a better.

Some time ago a correspondent to the *Spectator* stated : " As you are not one to despise ' unconsidered trifles ' when they have merit, perhaps you will find room for the following epitaph, on a Deal Boatman,

EPITAPHS ON SOLDIERS AND SAILORS. 79

which I copied the other day from a tombstone in a churchyard in that town :—

> In Memory of GEORGE PHILLPOT,
> Who died March 22nd, 1850, aged 74 years.
> Full many a life he saved
> With his undaunted crew;
> *He put his trust in Providence,*
> AND CARED NOT HOW IT BLEW.

A hero ; his heroic life and deeds, and the philosophy of religion, perfect both in theory and practice, which inspired them, all described in four lines of graphic and spirited verse! Would not 'rare Ben' himself have acknowledged this a good specimen of 'what verse can say in a little?' Whoever wrote it was a poet 'with the name.'"

There is another in the same churchyard, which though weak after the above, and indeed not uncommon, I fancy, in seaside towns, is at least sufficiently quaint:—

In Memory of JAMES EPPS BUTTRESS, who, in rendering assistance to the French Schooner, "Vesuvienne," was drowned, December 27th, 1852, aged 39.

> Though Boreas' blast and Neptune's wave
> Did toss me to and fro,
> In spite of both, by God's decree,
> I harbour here below ;
> And here I do at anchor ride
> With many of our fleet,
> Yet once again I must set sail,
> Our Admiral, Christ, to meet.

Also two sons, who died in infancy, &c.

The 'human race' typified by '*our fleet*,' excites vague reminiscences of Goethe and Carlyle, and 'our Admiral Christ' seems not remotely associated in sentiment with the 'We fight that fight for our fair father Christ,' and 'The King will follow Christ and we the King,' of our grand poet. So do the highest and the lowest meet. But the heartiness, the vitality, nay, almost vivacity, of some of these underground tenantry is surprising. There is more life in some of our dead folk than in many a living crowd."

We copied the following five epitaphs from Hessle-road cemetery, Hull :—

> WILLIAM EASTON,
> Who was lost at sea,
> In the fishing smack Martha,
> In the gale of January, 1865.
> Aged 30 years.

When through the torn sail the wild tempest is streaming ;
When o'er the dark wave the red lightning is gleaming,
No hope lends a ray the poor fisher to cherish.
Oh hear, kind Jesus ; save, Lord, or we perish !

> In affectionate remembrance of
> THOMAS CRACKLES,
> Humber Pilot, who was drowned off
> The Lincolnshire Coast,
> During the gale, October 19th, 1869.
> Aged 24 years.

How swift the torrent rolls
That hastens to the sea ;
How strong the tide that bears our souls
    On to Eternity.

In affectionate remembrance of
DAVID COLLISON,
Who was drowned in the " Spirit of the Age,"
Off Scarborough, Jan. 6th, 1864.
Aged 36 years.

I cannot bend over his grave,
  He sleeps in the secret sea ;
And not one gentle whisp'red wave
  Can tell that place to me.

Although unseen by human eyes,
  And mortal know'd it not ;
Yet Christ knows where his body lies,
  And angels guard the spot.

ROBERT PICKERING, who was
Drowned from the smack " Satisfaction,"
On the Dutch coast, May 7, 1869.
Aged 18 years.

The waters flowed on every side,
  No chance was there to save ;
At last compelled, he bowed and died,
  And found a watery grave.

In affectionate remembrance of
WILLIAM HARRISON,
53 years Mariner of Hull,
Who died October 5th, 1864.
Aged 70 years.

Long time I ploughed the ocean wide,
　A life of toil 1 spent ;
But now in harbour safe arrived
　From care and discontent.

My anchor's cast, my sails are furled,
　And now I am at rest.
Of all the parts throughout the world,
　Sailors, this is the best.

Our next example is copied from a stone which is so fast decaying that already some parts of the inscription are obliterated :—

Sacred
to the memory
of
WILLIAM WALKER,
. . . . . r of the Sloop Janatt,
. . . . who was unfortunately
drowned off Flamborough Head,
17th April, 1823.
Aged 41 years.

This stone was Erected by
his Countrymen in
remembrance of his Death.

I have left the troubled ocean,
And now laid down to sleep,
In hopes I shall set sail
Our Saviour Christ to meet.

A gravestone in Horncastle churchyard, Lincolnshire, has this epitaph :—

> My helm was gone,
> My sails were rent,
> My mast went by the board,
> My hull it struck upon a rock,
> Receive my soul, O Lord !

On a sailor's gravestone in the burial-ground at Hamilton, we are told :—

> The seas he ploughed for twenty years,
> Without the smallest dread or fears :
> And all that time was never known
> To strike upon a bank or stone.

PUNNING EPITAPHS.

PUNS in epitaphs have been very common, and may be found in Greek and Latin, and still more plentifully in our English compositions. In the French, Italian, Spanish, Portuguese, Dutch, and other languages, examples may also be found. Empedrocles wrote an epitaph containing the paronomasia, or pun, on a physician named Pausanias, and it has by Merivale been happily translated :—

> Pausanias—not so nam'd without a cause,
> As one who oft has giv'n to pain a pause,
> Blest son of Æsculapius, good and wise,
> Here, in his native Gela, buried lies ;
> Who many a wretch once rescu'd by his charms
> From dark Persephone's constraining arms.

In Holy Trinity Church, Hull, is an example of a punning epitaph. It is on a slab in the floor of the north aisle of the nave, to the memory of " The Worshipful Joseph Field, twice Mayor of this town, and Merchant Adventurer." He died in 1627, aged 63 years:—

Here is a Field sown, that at length must sprout,
And 'gainst the ripening harvest's time break out,
When to that Husband it a crop shall yield
Who first did dress and till this new-sown Field;
Yet ere this Field you see this crop can give,
The seed first dies, that it again may live.
    Sit Deus amicus,
    Sanctis, vel in Sepulchris spes est.

On Bishop Theophilus Field, in Hereford Cathedral, ob. 1636, is another specimen:—

The Sun that light unto three churches gave
Is set; this Field is buried in a grave.
This Sun shall rise, this Field renew his flowers,
This sweetness breathe for ages, not for hours.

He was successively Bishop of Llandaff, St. David's, and Hereford.

The following rather singular epitaph, with a play upon the name, occurs in the chancel of Checkley Church, Staffordshire:—

To the Memory of the Reverend JAMES WHITEHALL, Rector of this place twenty and five years, who departed this life the second daie of March, 1644.

White was his name, and whiter than this stone.
In hope of joyfole resurrection
Here lies that orthodox, that grave divine,
In wisdom trve, vertve did soe clearly shine;
One that could live and die as he hath done
Suffer'd not death but a translation.
Bvt ovt of charitie I'll speake no more,
Lest his friends pine with sighs, with teares the poor.

From Hornsea Church we have the epitaph of Will Day, gentleman; he lived 34 years, died May 22nd, 1616:—

> If that man's life be likened to a day,
> One here interr'd in youth did lose a day,
> By death, and yet no loss to him at all,
> For he a threefold day gain'd by his fall;
> One day of rest is bliss celestial,
> Two days on earth by gifts terrestryall—
> Three pounds at Christmas, three at Easter Day,
> Given to the poure until the world's last day,
> This was no cause to heaven; but, consequent,
> Who thither will, must tread the steps he went.
> For why? Faith, Hope, and Christian Charity,
> Perfect the house framed for eternity.

On the east wall of the Chancel of Kettlethorpe Church, co. Lincoln, is a tablet to the memory of "Johannes Becke, quondam Rector istius ecclesiæ," who died 1597, with the following lines in old English characters:—

> I am a BECKE, or river as you know,
> And wat'red here ye church, ye schole, ye pore,
> While God did make my springes here for to flow:
> But now my fountain stopt, it runs no more;
> From Church and schole mi life ys now bereft,
> But no ye pore four poundes I yearly left.

We may add that the stream of his charity still flows, and is yearly distributed amongst the poor of Kettlethorpe.

Bishop Sanderson, in his "Survey of Lincoln Cathedral," gives the following epitaph of Dr. William Cole, Dean of Lincoln, who died in 1600. The upper part of the stone, with Dr. Cole's arms, is, or was lately, in the Cathedral, but the epitaph has been lost:—

> Reader, behold the pious pattern here
> Of true devotion and of holy fear.
> He sought God's glory and the churches good.
> Idle idol worship he withstood.
> Yet dyed in peace, whose body here doth lie
> In expectation of eternity.
> And when the latter trump of heaven shall blow
> Cole, now rak'd up in ashes, then shall glow.

Here is another from Lincoln Cathedral, on Dr. Otwell Hill:—

> 'Tis OTWELL HILL, a holy Hill,
>   And truly, sooth to say,
> Upon this Hill be praised still
>   The Lord both night and day.
> Upon this Hill, this HILL did cry
>   Aloud the scripture letter,
> And strove your wicked villains by
>   Good conduct to make better.
> And now this HILL, tho' under stones,
>   Has the Lord's Hill to lie on;
> For Lincoln Hill has got his bones,
>   His soul the Hill of Sion.

The *Guardian*, for 3rd Dec., 1873, gives the following epitaph as being in Lillington Church, Dorset, on the grave of a man named Cole, who died in 1669:—

Reader, you have within this grave
A Cole rak'd up in dust.
His courteous Fate saw it was Late,
And that to Bed he must.
Soe all was swept up to be Kept
Alive until the day
The Trump shall blow it up and shew
The Cole but sleeping lay.
Then do not doubt the Coles not out
Though it in ashes lyes,
That little sparke now in the Darke
Will like the Phœnyx rise.

Our next example was inscribed in Peterborough Cathedral, to the memory of Sir Richard Worme, ob. 1589 :—

Does Worm eat Worme? Knight Worme this truth confirms,
For here, with worms, lies Worme, a dish for worms.
Does worm eat Worme? sure Worme will this deny,
For Worme with worms, a dish for worms don't lie.
'Tis so, and 'tis not so, for free from worms
'Tis certain Worme is blest without his worms.

On a person named Cave, at Barrow-on-Soar, Leicestershire, we have the following epitaph:

Here, in this Grave, there lies a Cave.
  We call a Cave a Grave:
If Cave be Grave, and Grave be Cave,
  Then, reader, judge, I crave,
Whether doth Cave here lie in Grave
  Or Grave here lie in Cave:
If Grave in Cave here buried lie,
Then Grave, where is thy victory?
Go reader, and report, here lies a Cave,
Who conquers Death, and buries his own Grave.

In Bletchley, ob. 1615, on Mrs. Rose Sparke :—

> Sixty-eight years a fragrant Rose she lasted,
> Noe vile reproach her virtues ever blasted ;
> Her autume past expects a glorious springe,
> A second better life more flourishing.

Hearken unto me, ye holy children, and bud forth as a Rose.—
Eccles. xxxix., 13.

From several punning epitaphs on the name of Rose we give one more specimen. It is from Tawton Church, ob. 1652, on Rose Dart :—

> A Rose springing Branch no sooner bloom'd,
> By Death's impartial Dart lyes here entombed.
> Tho' wither'd be the Bud, the stock relyes
> On Christ, both sure by Faith and Hope to rise.

In Barnstaple Church, ob. 1627, on Grace Medford, is an epitaph as follows :—

> Scarce seven years old this Grace in glory ends,
> Nature condemns, but Grace the change commends ;
> For Gracious children, tho' they die at seven,
> Are heirs-apparent to the Court of Heaven.
> Then grudge not nature at so short a Race ;
> Tho' short, yet sweet, for surely 'twas God's Grace.

On a punster the following was written :—

> Beneath the gravel and these stones,
> Lies poor JACK TIFFEY's skin and bones ;
> His flesh I oft have heard him say,
> He hoped in time would make good hay ;
> Quoth I, "How can that come to pass ?"
> And he replied, "All flesh is grass !"

EPITAPHS ON MUSICIANS AND ACTORS.

 A FEW epitaphs relating to music and the drama now claim our attention. Our first example is to be found in the cathedral at Norwich:—

> Here WILLIAM INGLOTT, organist, doth rest,
> Whose art in musick this Cathedral blest;
> For descant most, for voluntary all,
> He past on organ, song, and virginall.
> He left this life at age of sixty-seven,
> And now 'mongst angels all sings St. in Heaven;
> His fame flies far, his name shall never die,
> See, art and age here crown his memorie.
>> *Non digitis, Inglotte, tuis terrestria tangis,*
>> *Tangis nunc digitis organa celsa poli.*
>>> Anno Dom. 1621.

| Buried the last day | This erected the 15th |
| of December, 1621. | day of June, 1622. |

In Wakefield parish church a tablet bears an inscription as follows:—

In memory of
HENRY CLEMETSHAW,
upwards of fifty years organist
of this church, who died
May 7, 1821, aged 68 years.

Now, like an organ, robb'd of pipes and breath,
Its keys and stops are useless made by death,
Tho' mute and motionless in ruins laid ;
Yet when re-built by more than mortal aid,
This instrument, new voiced, and tuned, shall raise,
To God, its builder, hymns of endless praise.

We copy the following from a monument in Holy Trinity Church, Hull :—

In memory of
GEORGE LAMBERT,
late Organist of this Church,
which office he held upwards of 40 years,
performing its duties with ability
and assiduity rarely exceeded,
affording delight to the lovers
of Sacred Harmony,
This Tablet is erected
by his Musical and private Friends,
aided by the brothers of the Humber
and Minerva Lodges of Free Masons of this Town
(being a member of the latter Lodge),
That they might place on record
the high sense they entertained
of his personal and professional merit.
He died Feb. 19th, 1838, aged 70 years,
And his Remains were interred at the
Parish Church of St. John in Beverley.

> Tho' like an Organ now in ruins laid,
> Its stops disorder'd and its frame decay'd,
> This instrument ere long new tun'd shall raise
> To God, its Builder, notes of endless praise.

From a churchyard in Wales we obtain the following curious epitaph on an organ blower :—

> Under this stone lies MEREDITH MORGAN,
> Who blew the bellows of our church organ.
> Tobacco he hated, to smoke most unwilling,
> Yet never so pleased as when *pipes* he was filling.
> No reflection on him for rude speech could be cast,
> Though he gave our old organ many a blast !
> No puffer was he, though a capital blower ;
> He could blow double G, and now lies a note lower.

Our next epitaph records the death of a fiddler, who appears to have been so much attached to his wife that upon the day of her death he, too, yielded to the grim tyrant. Of this pair, buried in Flixton churchyard, it may be truly said : ' In life united, and in death not parted.' The inscription is as follows :—

To the Memory of JOHN BOOTH, of Flixton, who died 16th March, 1778, aged 43 years ; on the same day and within a few hours of the death of his wife HANNAH, who was buried with him in the same grave, leaving seven children behind them.

> Reader, have patience, for a Moment Stay,
>   Nor grudge the Tribute of a friendly tear,
> For John, who once made all our Village gay,
>   Has taken up his Clay-cold Lodging here.

Suspended now his fiddle lies asleep,
  That once with Musick us'd to charm the Ear.
Not for his Hannah long reserv'd to weep,
  John yields to Fate with his companion dear.

So tenderly he loved his dearer part,
  His Fondness could not bear a stay behind ;
And Death through Kindness seem'd to throw the dart
  To ease his sorrow, as he knew his mind.

In cheerful Labours all their Time they spent,
  Their happy Lives in Length of Days acquir'd ;
But Hand in Hand to Nature's God they went,
  And just lay down to sleep when they were tir'd.

The Relicks of this faithful, honest Pair
  One little Space of Mother Earth contains.
Let Earth protect them with a Mother's Care,
  And Constant Verdure grace her for her pains.

The Pledges of their tender loves remain,
  For seven fine children bless'd their nuptial State.
Behold them, neighbours ! nor behold in vain,
  But heal their Sorrows and their lost Estate.'

In the Old Cemetery, Newport, Monmouthshire, on a Scotch Piper, the following appears :—

To the memory of Mr. JOHN MACBETH, late piper to His Grace the Duke of Sutherland, and a native of the Highlands of Scotland :
Died April 24th, 1852, Aged 46 years.

Far from his native land, beneath this stone,
Lies JOHN MACBETH, in prime of manhood gone ;
A kinder husband never yet did breathe,
A firmer friend ne'er trod on Albyn's heath ;

His selfish aims were all in heart and hand,
To be an honour to his native land,
As real Scotchmen wish to fall or stand.
A handsome *Gael* he was, of splendid form,
Fit for a siege, or for the Northern Storm,
Sir Walter Scott remarked at Inverness,
" How well becomes Macbeth the Highland dress !"
His mind was stored with ancient Highland lore ;
Knew Ossian's songs, and many bards of yore ;
But music was his chief, and soul's delight.
And oft he played, with Amphion's skill and might,
His Highland pipe, before our Gracious Queen !
'Mong Ladies gay, and Princesses serene !
His magic chanter's strains pour'd o'er their hearts,
With thrilling rapture soft as Cupid's darts !
Like Shakespeare's witches, scarce they drew the breath,
But wished, like them, to say, " All hail, Macbeth !
The Queen, well pleased, gave him by high command,
A splendid present from her Royal hand !
But nothing aye could make him vain or proud,
He felt alike at Court or in a crowd ;
With high and low his nature was to please,
Frank with the Peasant, with the Prince at ease.
Beloved by thousands till his race was run,
Macbeth had ne'er a foe beneath the sun ;
And now he plays among the Heavenly bands,
A diamond chanter never made with hands.

In the church of Ashover, Derbyshire, a tablet contains this inscription :—

To the Memory of
DAVID WALL,

whose superior performance on the
bassoon endeared him to an
extensive musical acquaintance.
His social life closed on the
4th Dec., 1796, in his 57th year.

The next is copied from a gravestone in Stony Middleton churchyard:—

In memory of GEORGE, the son of GEORGE and MARGARET SWIFT, of Stoney Middleton, who departed this life August the 21st, 1759, in the 20th year of his age.

We the Quoir of Singers of this Church have erected this stone.
> He's gone from us, in more seraphick lays
> In Heaven to chant the Great Jehovah's praise ;
> Again to join him in those courts above,
> Let's here exalt God's name with mutual love.

The following was written in memory of Madame Malibran, who died September 23rd, 1836 :—

"The beautiful is vanished, and returns not."

'Twas but as yesterday, a mighty throng,
    Whose hearts, as one man's heart, thy power could bow,
Amid loud shoutings hailed thee queen of song,
    And twined sweet summer flowers around thy brow ;
And those loud shouts have scarcely died away,
    And those young flowers but half forgot thy bloom,
When thy fair crown is changed for one of clay—
    Thy boundless empire for a narrow tomb !
Sweet minstrel of the heart, we list in vain
    For music now ; THY melody is o'er ;
Fidelio hath ceased o'er hearts to reign,
    Somnambula hath slept to wake no more !
Farewell ! thy sun of life too soon hath set,
    But memory shall reflect its brightness yet.

Garrick's epitaph in Westminster Abbey, reads:—

> To paint fair Nature by divine command,
> Her magic pencil in his glowing hand,
> A SHAKESPEARE rose ; then, to expand his fame
> Wide o'er the breathing world, a GARRICK came :
> Tho' sunk in death, the forms the poet drew
> The actor's genius bade them breathe anew ;
> Tho', like the bard himself, in night they lay,
> Immortal GARRICK call'd them back to day ;
> And till eternity, with power sublime,
> Shall mark the mortal hour of hoary time,
> SHAKESPEARE and GARRICK, like twin stars shall shine,
> And earth irradiate with beams divine.

A monument placed in Westminster to the memory of Mrs. Pritchard states :—

This Tablet is here placed by a voluntary subscription of those who admired and esteemed her. She retired from the stage, of which she had long been the ornament, in the month of April, 1768 : and died at Bath in the month of August following, in the 57th year of her age.

> Her comic vein had every charm to please,
> 'Twas nature's dictates breath'd with nature's ease ;
> Ev'n when her powers sustain'd the tragic load,
> Full, clear, and just, the harmonious accents flow'd,
> And the big passions of her feeling heart
> Burst freely forth, and show'd the mimic art.
> Oft, on the scene, with colours not her own,
> She painted vice, and taught us what to shun ;
> One virtuous tract her real life pursu'd,
> That nobler part was uniformly good ;
> Each duty there to such perfection wrought,
> That, if the precepts fail'd, the example taught.

On a comedian named John Hippisley, interred in the churchyard of Clifton, Gloucestershire, we have the following :—

> When the Stage heard that death had struck her John,
> Gay Comedy her Sables first put on ;
> Laughter lamented that her Fav'rite died,
> And Mirth herself, ('tis strange) laid down and cry'd.
> Wit droop'd his head, e'en Humour seem'd to mourn,
> And solemnly sat pensive o'er his urn.

Garrick's epitaph to the memory of James Quin, in Bath Cathedral, is very fine :—

> That tongue, which set the table in a roar,
> And charm'd the public ear, is heard no more ;
> Closed are those eyes, the harbingers of wit,
> Which spoke, before the tongue, what Shakespeare writ ;
> Cold are those hands, which, living, were stretch'd forth,
> At friendship's call, to succour modest worth.
> Here is JAMES QUIN ! Deign, reader to be taught,
> Whate'er thy strength of body, force of thought,
> In Nature's happiest mould however cast,
> " To this complexion thou must come at last."

We next give an actor's epitaph on an artist. In Chiswick churchyard is Garrick's epitaph on William Hogarth, (died Oct. 29, 1764, aged 67 years) as follows:—

> Farewell, great painter of mankind,
>   Who reach'd the noblest point of art,
> Whose pictured morals charm the mind,
>   And thro' the eye correct the heart.

If genius fire thee, reader, stay ;
  If nature touch thee, drop a tear ;
If neither move thee, turn away,
  For HOGARTH's honour'd dust lies here.

No marble pomp, or monumental praise,
My tomb, this dial—epitaph, these lays ;
Pride and low mouldering clay but ill agree ;
Death levels me to beggars—Kings to me.

Alive, instruction was my work each day ;
Dead, I persist instruction to convey ;
Here, reader, mark, perhaps now in thy prime,
The stealthy steps of *never-standing Time* :
Thou'lt be what I am—catch the present hour,
Employ that well, for that's within thy power.

In St. Mary's Church, Beverley, a tablet is placed in remembrance of a notable Yorkshire actor :—

> In Memory of
> SAMUEL BUTLER,
> A poor player that struts and
> frets his hour upon the stage, and
> then is heard no more.
> Obt. June 15th 1812,
> Æt. 62.

Butler's gifted son, Samuel William, was buried in Ardwick cemetery, Manchester. A gravestone placed to his memory bears the following eloquent inscription by Charles Swain :—

EPITAPHS ON MUSICIANS AND ACTORS. 99

Here rest the
mortal remains of
SAMUEL WILLIAM BUTLER,
Tragedian.
In him the stage lost a highly-gifted and accomplished actor,
one whose tongue the noblest creations
of the poet found truthful utterance.
After long and severe suffering he departed
this life the 17th day of July, in the year of
our Lord 1845. Aged 41 years.

Whence this ambition, whence this proud desire,
This love of fame, this longing to aspire?
To gather laurels in their greenest bloom,
To honour life and sanctify the tomb?
'Tis the Divinity that never dies,
Which prompts the soul of genius still to rise.
Though fade the Laurel, leaf by leaf away,
The soul hath prescience of a fadeless day;
And God's eternal promise, like a star,
From faded hopes still points to hopes afar;
Where weary hearts for consolation trust,
And bliss immortal quickens from the dust.
On this great hope, the painter, actor, bard,
And all who ever strove for Fame's reward,
Must rest at last; and all that earth have trod
Still need the grace of a forgiving God!

A very interesting sketch of the life of Butler, from the pen of John Evans, is given in the "Papers of the Manchester Literary Club" vol. iii, published 1877.

In many collections of epitaphs the following is stated to be inscribed on a gravestone at Gillingham, but we are informed by the Vicar that no such epitaph is to be found, nor is there any trace of it having been placed there at any time :—

Sacred

To the Memory of

THOMAS JACKSON, Comedian,

Who was engaged 21st of December, 1741, to play a comic cast of characters, in this great theatre—the world ; for many of which he was prompted by nature to excel.

The season being ended, his benefit over, the charges all paid, and his account closed, he made his exit in the tragedy of Death, on the 17th of March, 1798, in full assurance of being called once more to rehearsal ; where he hopes to find his forfeits all cleared, his cast of parts bettered, and his situation made agreeable, by Him who paid the great stock-debt, for the love He bore to performers in general.

The following epitaph was written by Swift on Dicky Pearce, who died 1728, aged 63 years. He was a famous fool, and his name carries us back to the time when kings and noblemen employed jesters for the delectation of themselves and their friends. It is from Beckley, and reads as follows :—

> Here lies the Earl of Suffolk's Fool,
>   Men call him DICKY PEARCE ;
> His folly serv'd to make men laugh,
>   When wit and mirth were scarce.
> Poor Dick, alas ! is dead and gone,
>   What signifies to cry ?
> Dickys enough are still behind
>   To laugh at by and by.

In our " Historic Romance," published 1883, by Hamilton, Adams, and Co., London, will be found an account of " Fools and Jesters of the English Sovereigns," and we therein state that the last recorded instance of a fool being kept by an English family, is that of John Hilton's Fool, retained at Hilton Castle, Durham, who died in 1746.

The following epitaph is inscribed on a tombstone in the churchyard of St. Mary Friars, Shrewsbury, on Cadman, a famous " flyer " on the rope, immortalised by Hogarth, and who broke his neck descending from a steeple in Shrewsbury, in 1740 :—

> Let this small monument record the name
> Of CADMAN, and to future times proclaim
> How, by an attempt to fly from this high spire,
> Across the *Sabrine* stream, he did acquire
> His fatal end. 'Twas not for want of skill,
> Or courage to perform the task, he fell ;
> No, no,—a faulty cord being drawn too tight
> Hurried his soul on high to take her flight,
> Which bid the body here beneath, good-night.

Joe Miller, of facetious memory, next claims our attention. We find it stated in Chambers's " Book of Days" (issued 1869), as follows : Miller was interred in the burial-ground of the parish of St. Clement Danes, in Portugal Street, where a tombstone was erected to his memory. About ten years ago, that burial-ground, by the removal of the mortuary remains, and the demolition of the monuments, was converted into a site for King's College Hospital. Whilst this not unnecessary, yet undesirable, desecration was in progress, the writer saw Joe's tombstone lying on the ground; and being told that it would be broken up and used as materials for the new building, he took an exact copy of the inscription, which was as follows:

'Here lye the Remains of
Honest Jo: MILLER,
who was
a tender Husband,
a sincere Friend,
. a facetious Companion,
and an excellent Comedian.
He departed this Life the 15th day of
August 1738, aged 54 years.

If humour, wit, and honesty could save
The humourous, witty, honest, from the grave,
The grave had not so soon this tenant found,
Whom honesty, and wit, and humour, crowned;
Could but esteem, and love preserve our breath,
And guard us longer from the stroke of Death,
The stroke of Death on him had later fell,
Whom all mankind esteemed and loved so well.
S. DUCK,
From respect to social worth,
mirthful qualities, and histrionic excellence,
commemorated by poetic talent in humble life.
The above inscription, which Time
had nearly obliterated, has been preserved
and transferred to this Stone, by order of
MR. JARVIS BUCK, Churchwarden,
. A. D. 1816.

JOE MILLER'S TOMBSTONE, ST. CLEMENT DANES CHURCHYARD, LONDON.

An interesting sketch of the life of JOE MILLER will be found in the "Book of Days," vol. II., page 216, and in the same informing and entertaining work, the following notes are given respecting the writer of the foregoing epitaph: "The 'S. DUCK,' whose name figures as author of the verses on MILLER'S tombstone, and who is alluded to on the same tablet, by Mr. Churchwarden Buck, as an instance of 'poetic talent in humble life,' deserves a short notice. He was a thresher in the service of a farmer near Kew, in Surrey. Imbued with an eager desire for learning, he, under most adverse circumstances, managed to obtain a few books, and educate himself to a limited degree. Becoming known as a rustic rhymer, he attracted the attention of Caroline, queen of George II., who, with her accustomed liberality, settled on him a pension of £30 per annum; she made him a Yeoman of the Guard, and installed him as keeper of a kind of museum she had in Richmond Park, called Merlin's Cave. Not content with these promotions, the generous, but perhaps inconsiderate queen, caused Duck to be admitted to holy orders, and preferred to the living of Byfleet, in Surrey, where he became a popular preacher among the lower classes, chiefly through the novelty of being the 'Thresher Parson.' This gave Swift occasion to write the following quibbling epigram :—

"The thresher Duck could o'er the queen prevail;
The proverb says,—'No fence against a flail.'

> From threshing corn, he turns to thresh his brains,
> For which her Majesty allows him grains;
> Though 'tis confest, that those who ever saw
> His poems, think 'em all not worth a straw.
> Thrice happy Duck! employed in threshing stubble!
> Thy toil is lessened, and thy profits double.

"One would suppose the poor thresher to have been beneath Swift's notice, but the provocation was great, and the chastisement, such as it was, merited. For though few men had ever less pretensions to poetical genius than Duck, yet the Court party actually set him up as a rival—nay, as superior—to Pope. And the saddest part of the affair was that Duck, in his utter simplicity and ignorance of what really constituted poetry, was led to fancy himself the greatest poet of the age. Consequently, considering that his genius was neglected, and that he was not rewarded according to his poetical deserts by being made the clergyman of an obscure village, he fell into a state of melancholy, which ended in suicide; affording another to the numerous instances of the very great difficulty of doing good. If the well-meaning queen had elevated Duck to the position of farm-bailiff, he might have led a long and happy life, amongst the scenes and the classes of society in which his youth had passed, and thus been spared the pangs of disappointed vanity and misdirected ambition."

Says a thoughtful writer, if truth, perspicuity, wit, gravity, and every property pertaining to the ancient or modern epitaph, were ever united in one of terse brevity, it was that made for Burbage, the tragedian, in the days of Shakespeare:—

"Exit BURBAGE."

Jerrold, perhaps, with that brevity, which is the soul of wit, trumped the above by his anticipatory epitaph on that excellent man and distinguished historian, Charles Knight:—

"Good KNIGHT."

EPITAPHS ON NOTABLE PERSONS.

WE have under this heading some curious graveyard gleanings on remarkable men and women. Our first is from a tombstone erected in the churchyard of Spofforth, at the cost of Lord Dundas, telling the remarkable career of John Metcalf, better known as " Blind Jack of Knaresborough ":—

> Here lies JOHN METCALF, one whose infant sight
> Felt the dark pressure of an endless night ;
> Yet such the fervour of his dauntless mind,
> His limbs full strung, his spirits unconfined,
> That, long ere yet life's bolder years began,
> The sightless efforts marked th' aspiring man ;
> Nor marked in vain—high deeds his manhood dared,
> And commerce, travel, both his ardour shared.
> 'Twas his a guide's unerring aid to lend—
> O'er trackless wastes to bid new roads extend ;
> And, when rebellion reared her giant size,
> ·'Twas his to burn with patriot enterprise ;
> For parting wife and babes, a pang to feel,
> Then welcome danger for his country's weal.
> Reader, like him, exert thy utmost talent given !
> Reader, like him, adore the bounteous hand of Heaven.

He died on the 26th of April, 1801, in the 93rd year of his age.

A few jottings respecting Metcalf, will probably be read with interest. At the age of six years he lost his sight by an attack of small-pox. Three years later he joined the boys in their bird-nesting exploits, and climbed trees to share the plunder. When he had reached thirteen summers he was taught music, and soon became a proficient performer; he also learned to ride and swim, and was passionately fond of field-sports. At the age of manhood it is said his mind possessed a self-dependence rarely enjoyed by those who have the perfect use of their faculties; his body was well in harmony with his mind, for when twenty-one years of age he was six feet one and a-half inches in height, strong and robust in proportion. At the age of twenty-five, he was engaged as a musician at Harrogate. About this time he was frequently employed during the dark nights as a guide over the moors and wilds, then abundant in the neighbourhood of Knaresborough. He was a lover of horse-racing, and often rode his own animals. His horses he so tamed that when he called them by their respective names they came to him, thus enabling him to find his own amongst any number and without trouble. Particulars of the marriage of this individual read like a romance. A Miss Benson, daughter of an innkeeper, reciprocated the affections of our hero; however, the suitor did not please the parents of the " fair lady," and they selected a Mr. Dickinson as her future husband. Metcalf, hearing that the object of his affection was to be married the following day to the young man selected by her father, hastened to free her by inducing the damsel to elope with him. Next day they were made man and wife, to the great surprise of all who knew them, and to the disappointment of the intended son-in-law. To all it was a matter of wonder how a handsome woman as any in the country, the pride of the place, could link her future with ' Blind Jack,' and, for his sake, reject the many good offers made her. But the bride set the matter at rest by declaring : " His actions are so singular, and his spirit so manly and enterprising, that I could not help it."

It is worthy of note that he was the first to set up, for the public accommodation of visitors to Harrogate, a four-wheeled chaise and a one-horse chair; these he kept for two seasons. He next bought horses and went to the coast for fish, which he conveyed to Leeds and Manchester. In 1745, when the rebellion broke out in Scotland, he joined a regiment of volunteers raised by Colonel Thornton, a patriotic gentleman, for the defence of the House of Hanover. Metcalf shared with his comrades all the dangers of the campaign. He was defeated at Falkirk, and victorious at Culloden. He was the first to set up (in 1754) a stage-waggon between York and Knaresborough, which he conducted himself twice a week in summer, and once a week in winter. This employment he followed until he commenced contracting for road-making. His first contract was for making three miles of road between Minskip and Ferrensby. He afterwards erected bridges and houses, and made hundreds of miles of roads in Yorkshire, Lancashire, Cheshire, and Derbyshire. He was a dealer in timber and hay, of which he measured and calculated the solid contents by a peculiar method of his own. The hay he always measured with his arms, and, having learned the height, he could tell the number of square yards in the stack. When he went out, he always carried with him a stout staff some inches taller than himself, which was of great service both in his travels and measurements. In 1778 he lost his wife, after thirty-nine years of conjugal felicity, in the sixty-first year of her age. She was interred at Stockport. Four years later he left Lancashire, and settled at the pleasant rural village of Spofforth, not far distant from the town of his nativity. With a daughter, he resided on a small farm until he died, in 1801. At the time of his decease, his descendants were four children, twenty grandchildren, and ninety great-grandchildren.

[In one of our articles in *Chambers's Journal* we furnished the foregoing sketch, and it has since been reproduced in many newspapers and in several volumes.]

In " Yorkshire Longevity," compiled by Mr. William Grainge, of Harrogate, a most painstaking writer on local history, will be found an interesting account of Henry Jenkins, a celebrated Yorkshireman. It is stated : "In the year 1743, a monument was erected, by subscription, in Bolton churchyard, to the memory of Jenkins ; it consists of a square base of freestone, four feet four inches on each side, by four feet six inches in height, surmounted by a pyramid eleven feet high. On the east side is inscribed :—

> This monument was
> erected by contribution,
> in ye year 1743, to ye memory
> of HENRY JENKINS.

On the west side :—

> HENRY JENKINS,
> Aged 169.

In the church, on a mural tablet of black marble, is inscribed the following epitaph, composed by Dr. Thomas Chapman, Master of Magdalen College, Cambridge :—

> Blush not, marble,
> to rescue from oblivion
> the memory of
> HENRY JENKINS :
> a person obscure in birth,
> but of a life truly memorable ;
> for
> he was enriched
> with the goods of nature,
> if not of fortune,
> and happy

in the duration,
if not variety,
of his enjoyments :
and,
tho' the partial world
despised and disregarded
his low and humble state,
the equal eye of Providence
beheld, and blessed it
with a patriarch's health and length of days :
to teach mistaken man,
these blessings were entailed on temperance,
or, a life of labour and a mind at ease.
He lived to the amazing age of 169 ;
was interred here, Dec. 6, (or 9,) 1670,
and had this justice done to his memory 1743.

This inscription is a proof that learned men, and masters of colleges, are not always exempt from the infirmity of writing nonsense. Passing over the modest request to the *black* marble not to blush, because it may *feel* itself degraded by bearing the name of the plebeian Jenkins, when it ought only to have been appropriated to kings and nobles, we find but questionable philosophy in this inappropriate composition.

The multitude of great events which took place during the lifetime of this man are truly wonderful and astonishing. He lived under the rule of nine sovereigns of England—Henry VII. ; Henry VIII. ; Edward VI. ; Mary ; Elizabeth ; James I. ; Charles I. ; Oliver Cromwell ; and Charles II. He was born when the

Roman Catholic religion was established by law. He saw the dissolution of the monasteries, and the faith of the nation changed—Popery established a second time by Queen Mary—Protestantism restored by Elizabeth—the Civil War between Charles and the Parliament begun and ended—Monarchy abolished—the young Republic of England, arbiter of the destinies of Europe—and the restoration of Monarchy under the libertine Charles II. During his time, England was invaded by the Scots; a Scottish King was slain, and a Scottish Queen beheaded in England; a King of Spain and a King of Scotland were Kings in England; three Queens and one King were beheaded in England in his days; and fire and plague alike desolated London. His lifetime appears like that of a nation, more than an individual, so long was it extended and so crowded was it with such great events."

The foregoing many incidents remind us of the well-known Scottish epitaph on Marjory Scott, who died February 26th, 1728, at Dunkeld, at the extreme age of one hundred years. According to Chambers's "Domestic Annals of Scotland," the following epitaph was composed for her by Alexander Pennecuik, but never inscribed, and it has been preserved by the reverend statist of the parish, as a whimsical statement of historical facts comprehended within the life of an individual :—

>Stop, passenger, until my life you read,
>The living may get knowledge from the dead.

> Five times five years I led a virgin life,
> Five times five years I was a virtuous wife;
> Ten times five years I lived a widow chaste,
> Now tired of this mortal life I rest.
> Betwixt my cradle and my grave hath been
> Eight mighty kings of Scotland and a queen.
> Full twice five years the Commonwealth I saw,
> Ten times the subjects rise against the law;
> And, which is worse than any civil war,
> A king arraigned before the subject's bar.
> Swarms of sectarians, hot with hellish rage,
> Cut off his royal head upon the stage.
> Twice did I see old prelacy pulled down,
> And twice the cloak did sink beneath the gown.
> I saw the Stuart race thrust out; nay, more,
> I saw our country sold for English ore;
> Our numerous nobles, who have famous been,
> Sunk to the lowly number of sixteen.
> Such desolation in my days have been,
> I have an end of all perfection seen!

A foot-note states: "The minister's version is here corrected from one of the *Gentleman's Magazines* for January 1733; but both are incorrect, there having been during 1728 and the one hundred preceding years no more than six kings of Scotland."

In Scott's "Tales of a Grandfather," there is an account of the Battle of Lillyard's Edge, which was fought in 1545. The spot on which the battle occurred is so called from an Amazonian Scottish woman, who is reported, by tradition, to have distinguished herself in the fight. An inscription which was placed on her tombstone was legible within the present century, and is said to have run thus :—

Fair Maiden Lillyard lies under this stane,
Little was her stature, but great was her fame ;
Upon the English louns she laid mony thumps,
And when her legs were cutted off, she fought upon her stumps.

The tradition says that a beautiful young lady, called Lillyard, followed her lover from the little village of Maxton, and when she saw him fall in battle, rushed herself into the heat of the fight, and was killed, after slaying several of the English.

On one of the buttresses on the south side of St. Mary's Church, at Beverley, is an oval tablet, to commemorate the fate of two Danish soldiers, who, during their voyage to Hull, to join the service of the Prince of Orange, in 1689, quarrelled, and having been marched with the troops to Beverley, during their short stay there sought a private meeting to settle their differences by the sword. Their melancholy end is recorded in a doggerel epitaph, of which we give an illustration.

In the parish registers the following entries occur :—

1689, December 16.—Daniel Straker, a Danish trooper buried.
 ,, December 23.—Johannes Frederick Bellow, a Danish trooper, beheaded for killing the other, buried.

In a note from the Rev. Jno. Pickford, M.A., we are told : "The mode of execution was, it may be

TABLET AT ST. MARY'S CHURCH, BEVERLEY.

presumed, by a broad two-handed sword, such a one as Sir Walter Scott has particularly described in "Anne of Geierstein," as used at the decapitation of Sir Archibald de Hagenbach, "and which the executioner is described as wielding with such address and skill. The Danish culprit was, like the oppressive knight, probably bound and seated in a chair; but such swords as those depicted on the tablet could not well have been used for the purpose, for they are long, narrow in the blade, and perfectly straight."

We have in the "Diary of Abraham de la Pryme," the Yorkshire Antiquary, some very interesting particulars respecting the Danes. Writing in 1689, the diarist tells us: " Towards the latter end of the aforegoing year, there landed at Hull about six or seven thousand Danes, all stout fine men, the best equip'd and disciplin'd of any that was ever seen. They were mighty godly and religious. You would seldom or never hear an oath or ugly word come out of their mouths. They had a great many ministers amongst them, whome they call'd pastours, and every Sunday almost, ith' afternoon, they prayed and preach'd as soon as our prayers was done. They sung almost all their divine service, and every ministre had those that made up a quire whom the rest follow'd. Then there was a sermon of about half-an-houre's length, all *memoratim*, and then the congregation broke up. When they adminstered the sacrament, the ministre goes into the church and caused notice to be given thereof, then all come before, and he examined them one by one whether they were worthy to receive or no. If they were he admitted them, if they were not he writ their names down in a book, and bid them prepare against the next Sunday. Instead of bread in the sacrament, I observed that they used wafers about the bigness and thickness of a sixpence. They held it no sin to play at cards upon Sundays, and commonly did everywhere where they were suffered ; for indeed in many places the people would not abide the same, but took the cards from them. Tho' they loved strong drink, yet all the while I was amongst them, which was all this winter, I never saw above five or six of them drunk."

The diarist tells us that the strangers liked this country. It appears they worked for the farmers, and sold tumblers, cups, spoons, &c., which they had imported, to the English. They acted in the court-house a play in their own language, and realised a good sum of money by their performances. The design of the piece was " Herod's Tyranny—The Birth of Christ —The Coming of the Wise Men."

In Bolton churchyard, Lancashire, is a gravestone of considerable historical interest. It has been incorrectly printed in several books and magazines, but we are able to give a literal copy drawn from a carefully compiled " History of Bolton," by John D. Briscoe :—

JOHN OKEY,

The servant of God, was borne in London, 1608, came into this toune in 1629, married Mary, daughter of James Crompton, of Breightmet, 1635, with whom he lived comfortably 20 yeares, & begot 4 sons and 6 daughters. Since then he lived sole till the da of his death. In his time were many great changes, & terrible alterations—18 yeares Civil Wars in England, besides many dreadful sea fights—the crown or command of England changed 8 times, Episcopacy laid aside 14 yeares ; London burnt by Papists, & more stately built againe ; Germany wasted 300 miles ; 200,000 protestants murdered in Ireland, by the papists ; this toune thrice stormed—once taken, & plundered. He went throw many troubles and divers conditions, found rest, joy, & happines only in holines—the faith, feare, and loue of God in Jesus Christ. He died the 29 of Ap and lieth here buried, 1684. Come Lord Jesus, o come quickly. Holiness is man's happines.

[THE ARMS OF OKEY.]

We gather from Mr. Briscoe's history that Okey was a woolcomber, and came from London, to superintend some works at Bolton, where he married the niece of the proprietor, and died in affluence.

Bradley, the "Yorkshire Giant," was buried in the Market Weighton church, and on a marble monument the following inscription appears:—

In memory of
WILLIAM BRADLEY,
(Of Market Weighton,)
Who died May 30th, 1820,
Aged 33 years.
He Measured
Seven feet nine inches in Height,
and Weighed
twenty-seven stones.

In " Celebrities of the Yorkshire Wolds," by Frederick Ross, an interesting sketch of Bradley is given. Mr Ross states that he was a man of temperate habits, and never drank anything stronger than water, milk, or tea, and was a very moderate eater.

In Hampsthwaite churchyard was interred a " Yorkshire Dwarf." Her gravestone states :—

In memory of JANE RIDSDALE, daughter of George and Isabella Ridsdale, of Hampsthwaite, who died at Swinton Hall, in the parish of Masham, on the 2nd day of January, 1828, in the 59th year of her age. Being in stature only 31½ inches high.

> Blest be the hand divine which gently laid
> My head at rest beneath the humble shade ;
> Then be the ties of friendship dear ;
> Let no rude hand disturb my body here.

In the burial-ground of St. Martin's, Stamford, Lincolnshire, is a gravestone to Lambert of surprising corpulency :—

> In remembrance of that prodigy in nature,
> DANIEL LAMBERT,
> a native of Leicester,
> who was possessed of an excellent and convivial mind, and
> in personal greatness had no competitor.
> He measured three feet one inch round the leg, nine feet four
> inches round the body, and weighed 52 stones 11lbs.
> (14lb. to the stone).
> He departed this life on the 21st of June, 1809, aged 39 years.
> As a testimony of respect, this stone was erected by his
> friends in Leicester.

Respecting the burial of Lambert we gather from a sketch of his life the following particulars : " His coffin, in which there was a great difficulty to place him, was six feet four inches long, four feet four inches wide, and two feet four inches deep ; the immense substance of his legs made it necessarily a square case. This coffin, which consisted of 112 superficial feet of elm, was built on two axle-trees, and four cog-wheels. Upon these his remains were rolled into his grave, which was in the new burial ground at the back of St. Martin's Church. A regular descent was made by sloping it for some distance. It was found necessary to take down the window and wall of the room in which he lay to allow of his being taken away."

In St. Peter's churchyard, Isle of Thanet, a gravestone bears the following inscription :—

In memory of Mr. RICHARD JOY called the
Kentish Samson
Died May 18th 1742 aged 67
Hercules Hero Famed for Strength
At last Lies here his Breadth and Length
See how the mighty man is fallen
To Death ye strong and weak are all one
And the same Judgment doth Befall
Goliath Great or David small.

Joy was invited to Court to exhibit his remarkable feats of strength. In 1699 his portrait was published, and appended to it was an account of his prodigious physical power.

The next epitaph is from St. James's cemetery, Liverpool :—

> Reader pause. Deposited beneath are the remains of
> SARAH BIFFIN,
> who was born without arms or hands, at Quantox Head, County of Somerset, 25th of October, 1784, died at Liverpool, 2nd October, 1850. Few have passed through the vale of life so much the child of hapless fortune as the deceased : and yet possessor of mental endowments of no ordinary kind. Gifted with singular talents as an Artist, thousands have been gratified with the able productions of her pencil ! whilst versatile conversation and agreeable manners elicited the admiration of all. This tribute to one so universally admired is paid by those who were best acquainted with the character it so briefly portrays. Do any inquire otherwise—the answer is supplied in the solemn adomonition of the Apostle—
>
>> Now no longer the subject of tears,
>> Her conflict and trials are o'er,
>> In the presence of God she appears
>>
>> . . . . .

Our correspondent, Mrs. Charlotte Jobling, from whom we received the above, says : " The remainder is buried· It stands against the wall, and does not appear to now mark the grave of Miss Biffin." Mr. Henry Morley, in his carefully prepared and entertaining " Memoirs of Bartholomew Fair," writing about the fair of 1799, mentions Miss Biffin. " She was found," says Mr. Morley, " in the Fair, and assisted by the Earl of Morton, who sat for his likeness to her, always taking the unfinished picture away with him when he left, that he might prove it to be all the work of her own shoulder. When it was done he laid it before George III., in the year 1808; obtained the King's favour for Miss Biffin; and caused her to receive, at his own expense, further instruction in her art from Mr. Craig. For the last twelve years of his life he maintained a correspondence with her; and, after having enjoyed favour from two King Georges, she received from William IV. a small pension, with which, at the Earl's request, she retired from a life among caravans. But fourteen years later, having been married in the interval, she found it necessary to resume, as Mrs. Wright, late Miss Biffin, her business as a skilful miniature painter, in one or two of our chief provincial towns."

The following on Butler, the author of " Hudibras," merits a place in our pages. The first inscription is from St. Paul's, Covent Garden :—

BUTLER, the celebrated author of " Hudibras," was buried in this church. Some of the inhabitants, understanding that so famous a man was there buried, and regretting that neither stone nor inscription recorded the event, raised a subscription for the purpose of erecting something to his memory. Accordingly, an elegant tablet has been put up in the portico of the church, bearing a medallion of that great man, which was taken from his monument in Westminster Abbey.

The following lines were contributed by Mr. O'Brien, and are engraved beneath the medallion :—

> A few plain men, to pomp and pride unknown,
> O'er a poor bard have rais'd this humble stone,

> Whose wants alone his genius could surpass,
> Victim of zeal ! the matchless " Hudibras."
> What, tho' fair freedom suffer'd in his page,
> Reader, forgive the author—for the age.
> How few, alas! disdain to cringe and cant,
> When 'tis the mode to play the sycophant.
> But oh ! let all be taught, from BUTLER's fate,
> Who hope to make their fortunes by the great ;
> That wit and pride are always dangerous things,
> And little faith is due to courts or kings.

The erection of the above monument was the occasion of this very good epigram by Mr. S. Wesley :—

> Whilst BUTLER (needy wretch !) was yet alive,
> No gen'rous patron would a dinner give ;
> See him, when starv'd to death and turn'd to dust,
> Presented with a monumental bust !
> The poet's fate is here in emblem shown,
> He ask'd for bread, and he received a stone.

It is worth remarking that the poet was starving, while his prince, Charles II., always carried a " Hudibras " in his pocket.

The inscription on his monument in the Abbey is as follows :—

Sacred to the Memory of
SAMUEL BUTLER,

Who was born at Strensham, in Worcestershire, 1612, and died at London, 1680 ; a man of uncommon learning, wit, and probity : as admirable for the product of his genius, as unhappy in the rewards of them. His satire, exposing the hypocrisy and wickedness of the rebels, is such an inimitable piece, that, as he was the first, he may be said to be the last writer in his peculiar manner. That he, who, when living, wanted almost everything, might not, after death, any longer want so much as a tomb, John Barber, citizen of London, erected this monument 1721.

Here are a few particulars respecting an oddity, furnished by a correspondent: " Died, at High Wycombe, Bucks, on the 24th May, 1837, Mr. John Guy, aged 64. His remains were interred in Hughenden churchyard, near Wycombe. On a marble slab, on the lid of his coffin, is the following inscription:—

> Here, without nail or shroud, doth lie
> Or covered by a pall, JOHN GUY.
>
> Born May 17th, 1773.
> Died —— 24th, 1837.

On his grave-stone these lines are inscribed:—

> In coffin made without a nail,
>   Without a shroud his limbs to hide;
> For what can pomp or show avail,
>   Or velvet pall, to swell the pride.
> Here lies JOHN GUY beneath this sod,
>   Who lov'd his friends, and fear'd his God.

This eccentric gentleman was possessed of considerable property, and was a native of Gloucestershire. His grave and coffin were made under his directions more than a twelvemonth before his death; the inscription on the tablet on his coffin, and the lines placed upon his gravestone, were his own compositions. He gave all necessary orders for the conducting of his funeral, and five shillings were wrapped in separate pieces of paper for each of the bearers. The coffin was of singular beauty and neatness in workmanship, and looked more like a piece of tasteful cabinet work intended for a drawing-room, than a receptable for the dead.

Near the great door of the Abbey of St. Peter, Gloucester, says Mr. Henry Calvert Appleby, at the bottom of the body of the building, is a marble monument to John Jones, dressed in the robes of an alderman, painted in different colours. Underneath the effigy, on a tablet of black marble, are the following words:—

JOHN JONES, alderman, thrice mayor of the city, burgess of the Parliament at the time of the gunpowder treason; registrar to eight several Bishops of this diocese.

He died in the sixth year of the reign of King Charles, on the first of June, 1630. He gave orders for his monument to be raised in his lifetime. When the workmen had fixed it up, he found fault with it, remarking that the *nose was too red*. While they were altering it, he walked up and down the body of the church. He then said that he had himself almost finished, so he paid off the men, and died the next morning.

The next epitaph from Newark, Nottinghamshire, furnishes a chapter of local history:—

Sacred to the memory
Of HERCULES CLAY, Alderman of Newark,

Who died in the year of his Mayoralty,
Jan. 1, 1644.
On the 5th of March, 1643,
He and his family were preserved
By the Divine Providence
From the thunderbolt of a terrible cannon
Which had been levelled against his house
By the Besiegers,
And entirely destroyed the same.
Out of gratitude for this deliverance,
He has taken care
To perpetuate the remembrance thereof
By an alms to the poor and a sermon ;
By this means
Raising to himself a Monument
More durable than Brass.

The thund'ring Cannon sent forth from its mouth the devouring
    Flames
Against my Household Gods, and yours, O Newark.
The Ball, thus thrown, Involved the House in Ruin ;
But by a Divine Admonition from Heaven I was saved,
Being thus delivered by a strength Greater than that of Hercules,
And having been drawn out of the deep Clay,
I now inhabit the stars on high.
Now, Rebel, direct thy unavailing Fires at Heaven,
Art thou afraid to fight against God—thou
Who hast been a Murderer of His People ?
Thou durst not, Coward, scatter thy Flames
Whilst Charles is lord of earth and skies.

Also of his beloved wife
Mary (by the gift of God)
Partaker of the same felicity.

> Wee too made one by his decree
> That is but one in Trinity,
> Did live as one till death came in
> And made us two of one agen ;
> Death was much blamed for our divorce,
> But striving how he might doe worse
> By killing th' one as well as th' other,
> He fairely brought us both togeather,
> Our soules together where death dare not come,
> Our bodyes lye interred beneath this tomb,
> Wayting the resurrection of the just,
> O knowe thyself (O man), thou art but dust.*

It is stated that Charles II., in a gay moment asked Rochester to write his epitaph. Rochester immediately wrote :—

> Here lies the mutton-eating king,
>   Whose word no man relied on ;
> Who never said a foolish thing,
>   Nor ever did a wise one.

On which the King wrote the following comment :—

> If death could speak, the king would say,
>   In justice to his crown,
> His *acts* they were the minister's,
>   His words they were his own.

Our friend, Mr. Thomas Broadbent Trowsdale, F.R.H.S., who has written much and well in history, folk-lore, etc., tells us: "In the fine old church of Chepstow, Monmouthshire, nearly opposite the reading

---

* "Annals of Newark-upon-Trent," by Cornelius Brown, published 1879.

desk, is a memorial stone with the following curious acrostic inscription, in capital letters :—

> HERE SEPT. 9th, 1680,
> WAS BURIED
> A TRUE BORN ENGLISHMAN,
> Who, in Berkshire, was well known
> To love his country's freedom 'bove his own :
> But being immured full twenty year
> Had time to write, as doth appear—
>
> HIS EPITAPH.
>
> H ere or elsewhere (all's one to you or me)
> E arth, Air, or Water gripes my ghostly dust,
> N one knows how soon to be by fire set free ;
> R eader, if you an old try'd rule will trust,
> Y ou'll gladly do and suffer what you must.
>
> M y time was spent in serving you and you,
> A nd death's my pay, it seems, and welcome too ;
> R evenge destroying but itself, while I
> T o birds of prey leave my old cage and fly ;
> E xamples preach to the eye—care then, (mine says)
> N ot how you end, but how you spend your days.

This singular epitaph points out the last resting place of Henry Marten, one of the judges who condemned King Charles I. to the scaffold. On the Restoration, Marten was sentenced to perpetual imprisonment, Chepstow Castle being selected as the place of his incarceration. There he died in 1680, in the twenty-eighth year of his captivity, and seventy-eighth of his age. He was originally interred in the chancel of the church; but a subsequent vicar of Chepstow, Chest by name, who carried his petty party animosities even beyond the grave, had the dead man's dust removed, averring that he would not allow the body of a regicide to lie so near the altar. And so it was that Marten's memorial came to occupy its present position in the passage leading from the nave to the north aisle. We are told that one, Mr Downton, a son-in-law of this pusillanimous parson, touched to the quick by his relative's harsh treatment of poor Marten's inanimate remains, retorted by writing this satirical epitaph for the Rev. Mr. Chest's tombstone :—

> Here lies at rest, I do protest,
>   One CHEST within another !
> The chest of wood was very good,—
>   Who says so of the other ?

Some doubt has been thrown on the probability of a man of Marten's culture having written, as is implied in the inscription, the epitaph which has a place on his memorial.

The regicide was a son of Sir Henry Marten, a favourite of the first James, and by him appointed Principal Judge of the Admiralty and Dean of Arches. Young Henry was himself a prominent person during the period of the disastrous Civil War, and was elected Member of Parliament for Berkshire in 1640. He was, in politics, a decided Republican, and threw in his lot with the Roundhead followers of sturdy Oliver. When the tide of popular favour turned in Charles II.'s direction, and Royalty was reinstated, Marten and the rest of the regicides were brought to judgment for signing the death warrant of their monarch. The consequence, in Marten's case, was life-long imprisonment, as we have seen, in Chepstow Castle."

Next is a copy of an acrostic epitaph from Tewkesbury Abbey :—

Here lyeth the body of THOMAS MERRETT, of Tewkesbury, Barber-chirurgeon, who departed this life the 22nd day of October, 1699.

T hough only Stone Salutes the reader's eye,
H ere (in deep silence) precious dust doth lye,
O bscurely Sleeping in Death's mighty store,
M ingled with common earth till time's no more,
A gainst Death's Stubborne laws, who dares repine,
S ince So much Merrett did his life resigne.

M urmurs and Teares are useless in the grave,
E lse hee whole Vollies at his Tomb might have.
R est here in Peace ; who like a faithful steward,
R epair'd the Church, the Poore and needy cur'd ;
E ternall mansions do attend the Just,
T o clothe with Immortality their dust,
T ainted (whilst under ground) with wormes and rust.

Under the shadow of the ancient church of Bakewell, Derbyshire, is a stone containing a long inscription to the memory of John Dale, barber-surgeon, and his two wives, Elizabeth Foljambe and Sarah Bloodworth. It ends thus :—

Know posterity, that on the 8th of April, in the year of grace 1757, the rambling remains of the above JOHN DALE were, in the 86th yeare of his pilgrimage, laid upon his two wives.

> This thing in life might raise some jealousy,
> Here all three lie together lovingly,
> But from embraces here no pleasure flows,
> Alike are here all human-joys and woes;
> Here Sarah's chiding John no longer hears,
> And old John's rambling Sarah no more fears;
> A period's come to all their toylsome lives,
> The good man's quiet; still are both his wives.

The following is from St. Julian's church, Shrewsbury:—

The remains of HENRY CORSER of this parish, Chirurgeon, who Deceased April 11, 1691, and Annie his wife, who followed him the next day after:—

> We man and wife,
> Conjoined for Life,
> Fetched our last breath
> So near that Death,
> Who part us would,
> Yet hardly could.
> Wedded againe,
> In bed of dust,
> Here we remaine,
> Till rise we must.
> A double prize this grave doth finde,
> If you are wise keep it in minde.

In St. Anne's Churchyard, Soho, erected by the Earl of Orford (Walpole), in 1758, these lines were (or are) to be read:—

Near this place is interred
.THEODORE, King of Corsica,
Who died in this Parish
December XI., MDCCLVI.,
Immediately after leaving
The *King's Bench Prison*,
By the benefit of the *Act of Insolvency;*
In consequence of which
He *registered his Kingdom of Corsica
For the use of his Creditors !*

The grave—great teacher—to a level brings
Heroes and beggars, galley-slaves and kings!
But THEODORE this moral learned, ere dead;
Fate pour'd its lessons on his living head,
Bestow'd a kingdom, and denied him bread.

In the burial-ground of the Island of Juan Fernandez, a monument states :—

In Memory of
ALEXANDER SELKIRK,
Mariner,
A native of Largo, in the county of Fife, Scotland,
Who lived on this island, in complete
solitude, for four years and four months.
He was landed from the Cinque Ports galley, 96 tons,
18 guns, A.D. 1704, and was taken off in the
Duke, privateer, 12th February, 1709.
He died Lieutenant of H.M.S. Weymouth,
A.D. 1723, aged 47 years.
This Tablet is erected near Selkirk's look out,
By Commodore Powell-and the Officers
of H.M.S. Topaze, A.D. 1868.

It is generally believed that the adventures of Selkirk suggested to Daniel Defoe the attractive story of "Robinson Crusoe." In the "Dictionary of English Literature," by William Davenport Adams, will be found important information bearing on this subject.

In *Gloucester Notes and Queries* we read as follows: "Stout's Hill is the name of a house situated on high ground to the south of the Village of Uley, built in the style which, in the last century, was intended for Gothic, but which may be more exactly defined as the 'Strawberry Hill' style. In a house of earlier date lived the father of Samuel Rudder, the laborious compiler of the *History of Gloucestershire* (1779). He lies in the churchyard of Uley, on the south side of the chancel, and his grave-stone has a brass-plate inserted, which records a remarkable fact:—

Underneath lies the remains of ROGER RUTTER, *alias* RUDDER, eldest son of John Rutter, of Uley, who was buried August 30, 1771, aged 84 years, having never eaten flesh, fish, or fowl, during the course of his long life.

Tradition tells us that this vegetarian lived mainly on 'dump,' in various forms. Usually he ate 'plain dump:' when tired of plain dump, he changed his diet to 'hard dump;' and when he was in a special state of exhilaration, he added the variety of 'apple dump' to his very moderate fare."

On the gravestone of Richard Turner, Preston, a hawker of fish, the following inscription appears:—

Beneath this stone are deposited the remains of RICHARD TURNER, author of the word Teetotal, as applied to abstinence from all intoxicating liquors, who departed this life on the 27th day of October, 1846, aged 56 years.

In Mr. W. E. A. Axon's able and entertaining volume, " Lancashire Gleanings " (pub. 1883), is an interesting chapter on the " Origin of the Word 'Teetotal.'" In the same work we are told that Dr. Whitaker, the historian of Whalley, wrote the following epitaph on a model publican :—

Here lies the Body of
JOHN WIGGLESWORTH,
More than fifty years he was the
perpetual Innkeeper in this Town.
Withstanding the temptations of that dangerous calling,
he maintained good order in his
House, kept the Sabbath day Holy,
frequented the Public Worship
with his Family, induced his guests
to do the same, and regularly
partook of the Holy Communion.
He was also bountiful to the Poor,
in private as well as in public,
and, by the blessings of Providence
on a life so spent, died
possessed of competent Wealth,
Feb. 28, 1813,
aged 77 years.

The churchyard of Sutton Coldfield, Warwickshire, contains a gravestone bearing an inscription as follows :—

> As a warning to female virtue,
> And a humble monument of female chastity,
> This stone marks the grave of
> MARY ASHFORD,
> Who, in the 20th year of her age, having
> Incautiously repaired to a scene of amusement,
> Was brutally violated and murdered
> On the 27th of May, 1817.
>
> Lovely and chaste as the primrose pale,
> Rifled of virgin sweetness by the gale,
> Mary ! the wretch who thee remorseless slew
> Avenging wrath, who sleeps not, will pursue ;
> For though the deed of blood was veiled in night,
> Will not the Judge of all mankind do right ?
> Fair blighted flower, the muse that weeps thy doom,
> Rears o'er thy murdered form this warning tomb.

The writer of the foregoing epitaph was Dr. Booker, vicar of Dudley. The inscription is associated with one of the most remarkable trials of the present century. It will not be without interest to furnish a few notes on the case. One Abraham Thornton was tried at the Warwick assizes for the murder of Mary Ashford, and acquitted. The brother and next of kin of the deceased, not being satisfied with the verdict, sued out, as the law allowed him, an appeal against Thornton, by which he could be put on his trial again. The law allowed the appeal in case of murder, and it also gave option to the accused of having it tried by wager of law or by wager of battle. The brother of the unfortunate woman had taken no account of this, and accordingly, not only Mr. Ashford, but the judge, jury, and bar were taken greatly aback, and stricken with dismay when the accused, being requested to plead, took a paper from Mr. Reader, his counsel, and a pair of gloves, one of which he drew on, and, throwing the other on the ground, exclaimed, " Not guilty ; and I am ready to defend the same with my body !" Lord Ellenborough on the bench appeared grave, and the accuser looked amazed, so the court was adjourned to enable the judge to have an opportunity of conferring with his learned brethren. After several adjournments, Lord Ellenborough at last declared solemnly, but reluctantly, that wager of battle was still the law of the land, and that the accused had a right of appeal to it. To get rid of the law an attempt was made, by passing a short and speedy Act of Parliament, but this was ruled impossible, as it would have been *ex post facto*, and people wanted curiously to see the lists set up in the Tothill Fields. As Mr. Ashford refused to meet Thornton, he was obliged to cry " craven !" After that the appellor was allowed to go at large, and he could not be again tried by wager of law after having claimed his wager of battle. In 1819 an Act was passed to prevent any further appeals for wager of battle.

The following is copied from a gravestone in Saddleworth churchyard, and tells a painful story :—

Here lies interred the dreadfully bruised and lacerated bodies of WILLIAM BRADBURY and THOMAS his son, both of Greenfield, who were together savagely murdered, in an unusually horrible manner, on Monday night, April 2nd, 1832, old William being 84, and Thomas 46 years old.

> Throughout the land, wherever news is read,
> Intelligence of their sad death has spread ;
> Those now who talk of far-fam'd Greenfield's hills
> Will think of Bill i' Jacks and Tom o' Bills.
>
> Such interest did their tragic end excite
> That, ere they were removed from human sight,
> Thousands upon thousands daily came to see
> The bloody scene of the catastrophe.
>
> One house, one business, and one bed,
> And one most shocking death they had ;
> One funeral came, one inquest pass'd,
> And now one grave they have at last.

The following on a Hull character is from South Cave churchyard :—

> In memory of THOMAS SCATCHARD,
> Who dy'd rich in friends, Dec. 10, 1809.
> Aged 58 years.
> That Ann lov'd Tom, is very true,
> Perhaps you'll say, what's that to you.
> Who e'er thou art, remember this,
> Tom lov'd Ann, 't was that made bliss.

In Welton churchyard, near Hull, the next curious inscription appears on an old gravestone :—

Here lieth He ould JEREMY, who hath eight times maried been, but now in his ould Age, he lies in his cage, under The gras so Green, which JEREMIAH SIMPSON departed this life in the 84 yeare of his age, in the year of our Lord 1719.

Mr. J. Potter Briscoe favours us with an account of a famous local character, and a copy of his epitaph. According to Mr. Briscoe, Vincent Eyre was by trade a needle-maker, and was a firm and consistent Tory in politics, taking an active interest in all the party struggles of the period. His good nature and honesty made him popular among the poor classes, with whom he chiefly associated. A commendable trait in his character is worthy of special mention, namely, that, notwithstanding frequent temptations, he spurned to take a bribe from any one. In the year 1727 an election for a Member of Parliament took place, and all the ardour of Vin's nature was at once aroused in the interests of his favourite party. The Tory candidate, Mr. Borlase Warren, was opposed by Mr. John Plumtree, the Whig nominee, and, in the heat of the excitement, Vin emphatically declared that he should not mind dying immediately if the Tories gained the victory. Strange to relate, such an event actually occurred, for when the contest and the " chairing " of the victor was over, he fell down dead with joy, September 6th, 1727. The epitaph upon him is as follows :—

> Here lies VIN EYRE ;
> Let fall a tear
>   For one true man of honour ;
> No courtly lord,
> Who breaks his word,
>   Will ever be a mourner.

     In freedom's cause
     He stretched his jaws,
      Exhausted all his spirit,
     Then fell down dead.
     It must be said
      He was a man of merit.
     Let Freemen be
     As brave as he,
      And vote without a guinea ;
     VIN EYRE is hurled
     To t'other world,
     And ne'er took bribe or penny.
  True to his friend, to helpless parent kind,
  He died in honour's cause, to interest blind.
  Why should we grieve life's but an airy toy ?
  We vainly weep for him who died of joy.

We will next give some account of an eccentric Lincolnshire schoolmaster, named William Teanby, who resided for many years at Winterton. Respecting the early years of his career we have not been able to obtain any information. At the age of 30, he was engaged as a school-master in the vestry of Winterton church. He had many scholars, and continued teaching until he had attained a very advanced age. Some years before his death a gravestone was ordered, whereon he cut in ancient court hand the epitaph of his wife and children. From this slab he mostly took his food, and long before his death, placed on two pieces of wood, it served him for a table. After the epitaph of his wife and children, he left a vacancy for his own name and age, to be inserted by a friend, which was done at his death. The coffin in which he proposed being buried was used by him a considerable time as a cupboard. The old man retained perfect possession of his senses to the last, and at the age of 95 attended the Lincoln assizes, and gave away as curiosities, many circular pieces of paper for watches, not larger than half-a-crown, on which he had written the Lord's prayer and creed. He was habitually serious. Through attending his school in the church, he became familiar with the house of death ; in feasting from his stone slab, he enjoyed his meals from the very source which was afterwards to record the events of his life; and in what was his every day cupboard he now enjoys a peaceful and quiet rest. He passed away at the advanced age of 97. The tombstone bears the following lines :—

> To us grim death but sadly harsh appears,
> Yet all the ill we feel, is in our fears ;
> To die is but to live, upon that shore
> Where billows never beat, nor tempests roar ;
> For ere we feel its probe, the pang is o'er ;
> The wife, by faith, insulting death defies ;
> The poor man resteth in yon azure skies ;—
> That home of ease the guilty ne'er can crave,
> Nor think to dwell with God, beyond the grave ;—
> It eases lovers, sets the captive free,
> And though a tyrant he gives liberty.

The following lines also appear on the same stone :—

> Death's silent summons comes unto us all,
> And makes a universal funeral !—

Spares not the tender babe because it's young,
Youth too, and its men in years, and weak and strong!
Spares not the wicked, proud, and insolent,
Neither the righteous, just, nor innocent ;
All living souls, must pass the dismal doom
Of mournful death, to join the silent tomb.

The following lines to the memory of Thomas Stokes are from his gravestone in Burton churchyard, upon which a profile of his head is cut. He for many years swept the roads in Burton :—

>This stone
>was raised by Subscription
>to the memory of
>THOMAS STOKES,
>an eccentric, but much respected,
>Deaf and Dumb man,
>better known by the name of
>"DUMB TOM,"
>who departed this life Feb. 25th, 1837,
>aged 54 years.

What man can pause and charge this senseless dust
With fraud, or subtilty, or aught unjust ?
How few can conscientiously declare
Their acts have been as honourably fair ?
No gilded bait, no heart ensnaring need
Could bribe poor STOKES to one dishonest deed.
Firm in attachment to his friends most true—
Though Deaf and Dumb, he was excell'd by few.
Go ye, by nature form'd without defect,
And copy Tom, and gain as much respect.

Next we deal with an instance of pure affection. The churchyard of the Yorkshire village of Bowes contains the grave of two lovers, whose touching fate suggested Mallet's beautiful ballad of " Edward and Emma." The real names of the couple were Rodger Wrightson and Martha Railton. The story is rendered with no less accuracy than pathos by the poet :—

> Far in the windings of the vale,
>   Fast by a sheltering wood,
> The safe retreat of health and peace,
>   A humble cottage stood.
>
> There beauteous Emma flourished fair,
>   Beneath a mother's eye ;
> Whose only wish on earth was now
>   To see her blest and die.
>
> Long had she filled each youth with love,
>   Each maiden with despair,
> And though by all a wonder owned,
>   Yet knew not she was fair.
>
> Till Edwin came, the pride of swains,
>   A soul devoid of art ;
> And from whose eyes, serenely mild,
>   Shone forth the feeling heart.

We are told that Edwin's father and sister were bitterly opposed to their love. The poor youth pined away. When he was dying Emma, was permitted to see him, but the cruel sister would scarcely allow her to bid him a word of farewell. Returning home, she heard the passing bell toll for the death of her lover—

> Just then she reached, with trembling step,
>   Her aged mother's door—
> "He's gone!" she cried, "and I shall see
>   That angel face no more!"
>
> "I feel, I feel this breaking heart
>   Beat high against my side"—
> From her white arm down sunk her head;
>   She, shivering, sighed, and died.

The lovers were buried the same day and in the same grave. In the year 1848, Dr. F. Dinsdale, F.S.A., editor of the "Ballads and Songs of David Mallet," etc., erected a simple but tasteful monument to the memory of the lovers, bearing the following inscription:—

RODGER WRIGHTSON, junr., and MARTHA RAILTON, both of Bowes; buried in one grave, He died in a fever, and upon tolling his passing bell, she cry'd out My heart is broke, and in a few hours expired, purely thro' love, March 15, 1714-15. Such is the brief and touching record contained in the parish register of burials. It has been handed down by unvarying tradition that the grave was at the west end of the church, directly beneath the bells. The sad history of these true and faithful lovers forms the subject of Mallet's pathetic ballad of "Edwin and Emma." *

In St. Peter's churchyard, Barton-on-Humber, there is a tombstone with the following strange inscription:—

> Doom'd to receive half my soul held dear,
> The other half with grief, she left me here.
> Ask not her name, for she was true and just;
> Once a fine woman, but now a heap of dust.

---

* Black's "Guide to Yorkshire."

As may be inferred, no name is given; the date is 1777. A curious and romantic legend attaches to the epitaph. In the above year an unknown lady of great beauty, who is conjectured to have loved " not wisely, but too well," came to reside in the town. She was accompanied by a gentleman, who left her after making lavish arrangements for her comfort. She was proudly reserved in her manners, frequently took long solitary walks, and studiously avoided all intercourse. In giving birth to a child she died, and did not disclose her name or family connections. After her decease, the gentleman who came with her arrived, and was overwhelmed with grief at the intelligence which awaited him. He took the child away without unravelling the secret, having first ordered the stone to be erected, and delivered into the mason's hands the verse, which is at once a mystery and a memento. Such are the particulars gathered from " The Social History and Antiquities of Barton-on-Humber," by H. W. Ball, issued in 1856. Since the publication of Mr. Ball's book, we have received from him the following notes, which mar somewhat the romantic story as above related. We are informed that the person referred to in the epitaph was the wife of a man named Jonathan Burkitt, who came from the neighbourhood of Grantham. He had been *valet de chambre* to some gentleman or nobleman, who gave him a large sum of money on his marrying the lady. They came to reside at Barton, where she died in childbirth. Burkitt, after the death of his wife, left the town, taking the infant (a boy), who survived. In about three years he returned, and married a Miss Ostler, daughter of an apothecary at Barton. He there kept the King's Head, a public-house at that time. The man got through about £2000 between leaving Grantham and marrying his second wife.

On the north wall of the chancel of Southam Church is a slab to the memory of the Rev. Samuel Sands, who, being embarrassed in consequence of his extensive liberality, committed suicide in his study (now the hall of the rectory). The peculiarity of the inscription, instead of suppressing inquiry, invariably raises curiosity respecting it :—

Near this place was deposited, on the 23rd April, 1815, the remains of S. S., 38 years rector of this parish."

In Middleton Tyas Church, near Richmond, is the following :—

This Monument rescues from Oblivion
the Remains of the Reverend JOHN MAWER, D.D.,
Late vicar of this Parish, who died Nov. 18, 1763, aged 60.
As also of HANNAH MAWER, his wife, who died
Dec. 20th, 1766, aged 72.
Buried in this Chancel.
They were persons of eminent worth.
The Doctor was descended from the Royal Family
of Mawer, and was inferior to none of his illustrious

ancestors in personal merit, being the greatest
Linguist this Nation ever produced.
He was able to speak & write twenty-two Languages,
and particularly excelled in the Eastern Tongues,
in which he proposed to His Royal Highness
Frederick Prince of Wales, to whom he was firmly
attached, to propagate the Christian Religion
in the Abyssinian Empire ; a great & noble
Design, which was frustrated by the
Death of that amiable Prince ; to the great mortification of
this excellent Person, whose merit meeting with
no reward in this world, will, it's to be hoped, receive
it in the next, from that Being which Justice
only can influence.

MISCELLANEOUS EPITAPHS.

WE bring together under this heading a number of specimens that we could not include in the foregoing chapters of classified epitaphs.

Our example is from Bury St. Edmunds churchyard :—

Here lies interred the Body of
MARY HASELTON,
A young maiden of this town,
Born of Roman Catholic parents,
And virtuously brought up,
Who, being in the act of prayer
Repeating her vespers,
Was instantaneously killed by a
flash of Lightning, August 16th,
1785. Aged 9 years.

Not Siloam's ruinous tower the
victims slew,
Because above the many sinn'd
the few,
Nor here the fated lightning
wreaked its rage
By vengeance sent for crimes
matur'd by age.

For whilst the thunder's awful
voice was heard,
The little suppliant with its hands
uprear'd,
Addressed her God in prayers
the priest had taught,
His mercy craved, and His protection sought ;
Learn reader hence that wisdom
to adore,
Thou canst not scan and fear His
boundless power ;
Safe shalt thou be if thou perform'st His will,
Blest if he spares, and more blest
should He kill.

A lover at York inscribed the following lines to his sweetheart, who was accidentally drowned, December 24, 1796:—

> Nigh to the river Ouse, in York's fair city,
> Unto this pretty maid death shew'd no pity ;
> As soon as she'd her pail with water fill'd
> Came sudden death, and life like water spill'd."

An accidental death is recorded on a tombstone in Burton Joyce churchyard, placed to the memory of Elizabeth Cliff, who died in 1835:—

> This monumental stone records the name
> Of her who perished in the night by flame
> Sudden and awful, for her hoary head ;
> She was brought here to sleep amongst the dead.
> Her loving husband strove to damp the flame
> Till he was nearly sacrificed the same.
> Her sleeping dust, tho' by thee rudely trod,
> Proclaims aloud, prepare to meet thy God.

We are told that a tombstone in Creton churchyard states:—

> On a Thursday she was born,
> On a Thursday made a bride,
> On a Thursday put to bed,
> On a Thursday broke her leg, and
> On a Thursday died.

From Ashburton we have the following:—

> Here I lie, at the chancel door,
> Here I lie, because I'm poor ;
> The farther in, the more you pay,
> Here I lie as warm as they.

In the churchyard of Kirk Hallam, Derbyshire, a good specimen of a true Englishman is buried, named Samuel Cleater, who died May 1st, 1811, aged 65 years. The two-lined epitaph has such a genuine, sturdy ring about it, that it deserves to be rescued from oblivion:—

> True to his King, his country was his glory,
> When Bony won, he said it was a story.

A monument in Bakewell church, Derbyshire is a curiosity, blending as it does in a remarkable manner, business, loyalty, and religion:—

To the memory of MATTHEW STRUTT, of this town, farrier, long famed in these parts for veterinary skill. A good neighbour, and a staunch friend to Church and King. Being Churchwarden at the time the present peal of bells were hung, through zeal for the house of God, and unremitting attention to the airy business of the belfry, he caught a cold, which terminated his existence May 25, 1798, in the 68th year of his age.

In Tideswell churchyard, among several other singular gravestone inscriptions, the following occurs, and is worth reprinting:—

> In Memory of
> BRIAN, Son of JOHN and MARTHA HAIGH,
> who died 22nd December, 1795,
> Aged 17 years.
>
> Come honest sexton, with thy spade,
> And let my grave be quickly made ;
> Make my cold bed secure and deep,
> That, undisturbed, my bones may sleep,

Until that great tremendous day,
When from above a voice shall say,—
"Awake, ye dead, lift up your eyes,
Your great Creator bids you rise!"
Then, free from this polluted dust,
I hope to be amongst the just.

The old church of St. Mary's, Sculcoates, Hull, contains several interesting monuments, and we give a sketch of one, a quaint-looking mural memorial, having on it an inscription in short-hand. In Sheahan's "History of Hull," the following translation is given:—

In the vault beneath this stone lies the body of Mrs. JANE DELAMOTH, who departed this life, 10th January, 1761. She was a poor sinner, but not wicked without holiness, departing from good works, and departed in the Faith of the Catholic Church, in full assurance of eternal happiness, by the agony and bloody sweat, by the cross and passion, by the precious death and burial, by the glorious resurrection and ascension of Our Lord and Saviour Jesus Christ, Amen.

We believe that the foregoing is a unique epitaph, at all events we have not heard of or seen any other monumental inscription in short-hand.

The following curious epitaph is from Wirksworth, Derbyshire:—

Near this place lies the body of

PHILIP SHULLCROSS,

Once an eminent Quill-driver to the attorneys in this Town. He died the 17th of Nov. 1787, aged 67.

Viewing Philip in a moral light, the most prominent and remarkable features in his character were his zeal and invincible attachment to dogs and cats, and his unbounded benevolence towards them, as well as towards his fellow-creatures.

To THE CRITIC.

Seek not to show the devious paths Phil trode,
Nor tear his frailties from their dread abode,
In modest sculpture let this tombstone tell,
That much esteem'd he lived, and much regretted fell.

At Castleton, in the Peak of Derbyshire, is another curious epitaph, partly in English and partly in Latin, to the memory of an attorney-at-law named Micah Hall, who died in 1804. It is said to have been penned by himself, and is more epigrammatic than reverent. It is as follows :—

To
The memory of
MICAH HALL, Gentleman,
Attorney-at-Law,
Who died on the 14th of May, 1804,
Aged 79 years.

Quid eram, nescitis ;
Quid sum, nescitis ;
Ubi abii, nescitis ;
Valete.

This verse has been rendered thus :—

> What I was you know not—
> What I am you know not—
> Whither I am gone you know not—
> Go about your business.

In Sarnesfield churchyard, near Weobley, is the tombstone of John Abel, the celebrated architect of the market-houses of Hereford, Leominster, Knighton, and Brecknock, who died in the year 1694, having attained the ripe old age of ninety-seven. The memorial stone is adorned with three statues in kneeling posture, representing Abel and his two wives; and also displayed are the emblems of his profession—the rule, the compass, and the square—the whole being designed and sculptured by himself. The epitaph, a very quaint one, was also of his own writing, and runs thus :—

This craggy stone a covering is for an architector's bed ;
That lofty buildings raisèd high, yet now lyes low his head ;
His line and rule, so death concludes, are lockèd up in store ;
Build they who list, or they who wist, for he can build no more.

> His house of clay could hold no longer,
> May Heaven's joy build him a stronger.
>
> JOHN ABEL.
>
> Vive ut vivas in vitam æternam.

The following inscription copied from a monument at Darfield, near Barnsley, records a murder which occurred on the spot where the stone is placed :—

Sacred
To the Memory of
THOMAS DEPLEDGE,
Who was murdered at Darfield,
On the 11th of October, 1841.

At midnight drear by this wayside
A murdered man poor DEPLEDGE died,
The guiltless victim of a blow
Aimed to have brought another low,
From men whom he had never harmed
By hate and drunken passions warmed.
Now learn to shun in youth's fresh spring
The courses which to ruin bring.

The following singular verse occurs upon a tombstone contiguous to the chancel door in Grindon churchyard, near Leek, Staffordshire :—

Farewell, dear friends ; to follow me prepare ;
Also our loss we'd have you to beware,
And your own business mind. Let us alone,
For you have faults great plenty of your own.
Judge not of us, now We are in our Graves
Lest ye be Judg'd and awfull Sentence have ;
For Backbiters, railers, thieves, and liars,
Must torment have in Everlasting Fires.

Bibliography of Epitaphs.

Addison, Joseph. Westminster Abbey, the *Spectator*, Nos. 26 and 329.

Alden, Rev. Timothy. A Collection of American Epitaphs; New York, 1814, 12mo., 5 vols.

Andrews, William, F.R.H.S. Gleanings from Yorkshire Graveyards, *Yorkshire Magazine*, vol. 2, pp. 95-6; Epitaphs on Sportsmen, *Illustrated Sporting and Dramatic News*, July 24th and 31st, 1880. Curious Epitaphs, *Chambers's Journal*, vol. 55, pp. 570-572. Many articles in the *Argonaut, Eastern Morning News, Fireside, Hand and Heart, Hull Miscellany, Hull News, Long Ago, Newcastle Courant, Notes and Queries, Notes about Notts., Nottingham Daily Guardian, Oldham Chronicle, Press News, Reliquary, Whitaker's Journal, Yorkshireman*, and about fifty other London magazines and provincial newspapers.

Anthologia: A Collection of Ludicrous Epitaphs and Epigrams; 1807, 12mo.

Appleby, Henry Calvert, Hull. Shakespeare and Epitaphs. "Miscellanea," edited by William Andrews, F.R.H.S., pp. 28-32.

Archer, Capt. J. H. Lawrence. The Monumental Inscriptions of the British West Indies, from the earliest date, with Genealogical and Historical Annotations from original, local, and other sources, illustrative of the Histories and Genealogies of the 17th and 18th Centuries. London: Chatto and Windus, 1875, 4to.

<small>Capt. Archer collected these epitaphs during the years 1858 and 1864-5, in the colonies of Jamaica and Barbadoes. The above is a very interesting volume.</small>

Asiaticus: Sketches of Bengal, Epitaphs in Burial Grounds round Calcutta. Calcutta, 1803, 8vo, 2 parts in 1 vol.

Bancroft, Thos. Two Books of Epigrammes and Epitaphs, Dedicated to two Top Branches of Gentry: Sir Charles Shirley, Bart., and William Davenport, Esq. London: printed by J. Okes, for Matthew Walbancke, and are to be sold at his shop in Grayes-Inne-gate, 1639, 4to, 86 pp.

Barker, T. B. Abney Park Cemetery: a Complete Guide to every part of this beautiful Depository of the Dead; with Historical Sketches of Stoke Newington. London, n.d. [1869], 8vo.

[Benham, Mrs. Edward]. Among the Tombs of Colchester. Colchester: Benham and Co., 1880, 8vo, 76 pp.

Blacker, Rev. Beaver Henry, M.A. Monumental Inscriptions in the Parish Church of Cheltenham. London, 1877, 4to. Privately Printed.

Monumental Inscriptions in the Parish Church of Charlton Kings; with Extracts from the Registers, etc., 1871.

Blanchard, L. The Cemetery at Kensal Green: the Grounds and Monuments. London: 1843, 8vo.

Booth, Rev. John, M.A. Metrical Epitaphs, Ancient and Modern. London and Eton: Bickers and Son, 1868, 12mo., pp. xxiv-215.

Bowden, John, Stonemason of Chester. The Epitaph Writer; consisting of upwards of six hundred original Epitaphs; Moral, Admonitory, Humorous, and Satirical. London, 1791, 12mo.

[Boyd, Rev. A. K. H.] Concerning Churchyards; by A. K. H. B. *Fraser's Magazine*, vol. 58, pp. 47-59.

Boyd, H. S. Tributes to the Dead, in a series of Ancient Epitaphs translated from the Greek, 1826, 12mo.

Brown, James, Keeper of the Grounds, and author of the " Deeside Guide." The Epitaphs and Monumental Inscriptions in Grey Friars' Churchyard, Edinburgh; collected by James Brown. Compiled and Edited [by J. Moodie Miller], with an Introduction by D[avid] L[aing, LL.D.] Edinburgh: J. Moodie Miller, 1867; 8vo, pp. lxxxiv-360, (and 23 illustrations.)

Caldwell, Thomas. A Select Collection of Ancient and Modern Epitaphs and Inscriptions. London, 1796, 12mo.

Cansick, Frederick Teague. A Collection of Curious and Interesting Epitaphs copied from the Monuments of Distinguished and Noted Characters in the Ancient Church and Burial Grounds of St. Pancras, Middlesex. London: J. R. Smith; 1869-72, 8vo, 2 vols.

Cemeteries, The, and Catacombs of Paris, *Quarterly Review*, vol. 21, pp. 359-398.

Churchyard Gleanings, or, a Collection of Epitaphs and Monumental Inscriptions. Derby: Published by Thomas Richardson; n.d., 8vo, 24 pp., and a large folding plate.

Churchyard Lyrist: consisting of five hundred original Inscriptions to commemorate the dead; 1832.

Churchyard, The Seaside. *Household Words*, vol. 2, pp. 257-262.

Churchyard Wanderings. *Colburn's New Monthly Magazine*, vol. 5, pp. 84-91.

Clark, Benjamin. Hand-book for Visitors to Kensal Green Cemetery. A new edition, with additions. London: Masters, 1843, 12mo., pp. xvi-108.

Clay, Edward. An History and Topographical Description of Framlingham, Interspersed with explanatory notes, poetical extracts, and translations of the Latin Inscriptions. Halesworth, n.d. [1810], 8vo, 144 pp., with two plates of the Castle.

Cobbe, Frances Power. French and English Epitaphs. *Temple Bar*, vol. 22, pp. 349-357.

Collinson, G. Cemetery Interments. London: Longman, 1840.

Counties of England, The, and their Quaint Old Lays and Epitaphs. *Tait's Edinburgh Magazine*, N. S., vol. 26, pp. 399-400.

The epitaphs in this article are collected from "Ye New and Complete British Traveller."

Croft, H. J., Guide to Kensal Green Cemetery, new edition. London, 1867, 8vo.

Crull, Jodocus, M.D. The Antiquities of St. Peter's, or the Abbey Church of Westminster: containing all the Inscriptions, Epitaphs, &c., upon the Tombs and Gravestones; London, 1711, 8vo. Second edition, London, 1715, 8vo; third edition, vol. 1, edited by H. S., vol. 2, by J. R., London, 1722, 8vo, 2 vols.; fourth edition, London, 1741, 8vo, 2 vols.; fifth edition, London, 1742, 8vo, 2 vols.

Dart, Rev. John. The History and Antiquities of the Cathedral Church of Canterbury, And the Once-Adjoining Monastery, &c.; London: Printed and sold by J. Cole, Engraver, at the Crown in Great Kirby St., Hatton Garden, and J. Hoddle, Engraver, in Bridewell Precinct, near Fleet Bridge, MDCCXXVI, fol., pp. ix-204; Appendix, pp. i-lvi, [With Illustrations.]

There is, in the above history, (pp. 39-91), a survey of the monuments in Canterbury Cathedral, with the inscriptions on the monuments and tombstones, and 27 plates.

[Diprose, John]. Diprose's Book of Epitaphs: Humorous, Eccentric, Ancient, and Remarkable. London: Diprose and Bateman, Lincoln's Inn Fields, n.d., [1879, 1880], 8vo, 80 pp.

Duncan, Andrew, M.D., M.P. Monumental Inscriptions selected from the Burial Grounds at Edinburgh; 1815, 8vo, 108 pp.

E., D. Stray Thoughts on Monumental Inscriptions. *Christian Observer*, vol. 6, pp. 609-619.

Epigrams and Epigraphs, by the author of " Proverbial Folk-Lore," n.d., 8vo, 176 pp.

Epitaph, *Encyclopædia Brittannica*, eighth edition, vol. 9, pp. 282-283; ninth edition, pp. 493-496.

———, *Penny Encyclopædia*, vol. 9, pp. 482-483.

Epitaphial Memorablia. *Dublin University Magazine*, vol. 55, pp. 580-585.

Epitaphs. *Chambers's Journal*, vol. 46, pp. 124-126.

———, Ancient and Modern,—*Chambers's Journal*, vol. 37, pp. 141-143.

———, Ancient and Modern in four parts; n.d., 8vo.

———, Bibliographical, *The Bibliographer*, vol. 1, pp. 81-82.

In this article there are epitaphs on Caxton, John Daye, Christopher Barker, John Foster, first printer of Boston, U.S., John Baskerville, Adam Williamson, and Rev. John Cotton.

Epitaphs, Collection of. and Inscriptions, 1802, 12mo.

———, Collection of, A, and Monumental Inscriptions. Historical, Biographical, Literary, and Miscellaneous; with an Essay by Samuel Johnson, LL.D, London: 1806, 12mo., 2 vols.

———, Collection, A, of Curious and Interesting, copied from the existing monuments of distinguished and noted characters in the Churches and Churchyards of Hornsey, Tottenham, Enfield, Edmonton, Barnet, and Hadley, in the county of Middlesex, 1875, 8vo, with plates and arms.

———, On, and Elegiac Inscriptions. *Dublin University Magazine*, vol. 40, pp. 206-212.

———, Original Collection, An, of Extant Epitaphs, gathered by a 'Commercial' in Spare Moments. London: Maiben, 1870, 8vo.

———, Original and Selected, with an Historical and Moral Essay on the subject; by a Clergyman, 1840, 8vo.

———, Scriptural, London: Smith and Elder, 1847, 18mo.

———, Select Collection of, A, not to be found in any other; dedicated to the Archbishops and Bishops. London, 1754, 8vo.

———, Some Curious, *Chambers's Journal*, vol. 57, pp. 666-668.

———, Traders,' *Chambers's Journal*, vol. 50, pp. 377-379.

——— and Epigrams. *The Norfolk Garland*, 1872, 8vo, pp. 142-147. [Epitaphs on W. Slater, the Yarmouth Stage Coachman, Micaiah Gage, Sir Thomas Hare, Bart., Beatrice, wife of John Guavor, John Dowe, Thomas Allyn and his two wives, Robert Gilbert, Prebendary J. Spendlove and his wife, Richard Corbet, D.D., William Inglott, Organist of Norwich Cathedral, Tom Page.]

BIBLIOGRAPHY OF EPITAPHS. 163

Epitaphs and Epigrams, Curious, Quaint, and Amusing, from various sources. London: Palmer, 1869, 12mo., 120 pp.

Fairley, W., F.S. S., Mining Engineer. Epitaphiana: or, The Curiosities of Churchyard Literature. Being a Miscellaneous Collection of Epitaphs. With an Introduction, giving an account of the various customs prevailing amongst the Ancients and Moderns in the Disposal of their Dead. London: Samuel Tinsley, 1873, 8vo, pp. viii-171.

Fisher, P., The Catalogue of most of the Memorable Tombes, Grave-stones, Plates, Escutcheons, or Atchievements in the demolisht or yet extant Churches of London, from St. Katherine's beyond the Tower to Temple Barre. London, 1668, 4to. There were two other editions of this work published in 1670, and 1684. The Tombes, Monuments, and Sepulchral Inscriptions, lately visible in St. Paul's Cathedral, and St. Faith's under it, completely rendered in Latin and English, with several discourses on sundry persons entombed therein. London, 1684, 4to.

Frobisher, Nathaniel. New Select Collection of Epitaphs; Humorous, Whimsical, Moral, and Satyrical. "The House appointed for all living," Job. [Round a view of a church and churchyard]. London: Printed for Nathaniel Frobisher, in the Pavement, York; n.d., [1790], 8vo, 216 pp., [With an engraved title].

Gardiner, Richard. An Elegy on the Death of Lady Asgill, Lady of Sir Charles Asgill, Knt., and Alderman of London; to which is added, An Epitaph on the late Sir Edmund Bacon, Bart., of Gillingham, in the county of Norfolk. London, 1754, fol.

Garrick, David. Epitaphs on Claudy Philips, A Lady's Bullfinch, A Clergyman, William Hogarth, James Quin, Sterne, Mr. Holland, Mr. Beighton, Whitehead, Howard. *Poetical Works*, 1785, 12mo., 2 vols., vol. 2, pp. 480-486.

Gibson, James. Inscriptions on the Tombstones and Monuments erected in Memory of the Covenanters. With Historical Introduction and Notes. Glasgow: Dunn and Wright, 176 Buchanan St., n.d. [1879], 12mo., pp. viii-291. [With five plates].

<small>The above interesting sketches were written for the *Ardrossan and Saltcoats Herald*, and appeared in that paper during the spring and summer of 1875.</small>

Graham, William. A Collection of Epitaphs and Monumental Inscriptions, Ancient and Modern; with an Emblematical Frontispiece, [Lanercost Priory, Camb]. Second edition; London: for T. and J. Allman, 1823, 8vo, pp. iv-320.

Hackett, John, late Commoner of Balliol College, Oxford. Select and Remarkable Epitaphs on Illustrious and other Persons in Several Parts of Europe. With Translations of such as are in Latin and Foreign Languages. And Compendious Accounts of the Deceased, their Lives and Works. London: Printed for T. Osborne and J. Shipton, in Gray's Inn, 1757, 8vo, 2 vols., pp. 288, 246, and Indexes, (22 pp.)

Hall-Stevenson, John. Works: containing Crazy Tales, Fables for grown Gentlemen, Lyric Epistles, Pastoral Cordial, Pastoral Puke, Macarony Fables, Monkish Epitaphs. London, 1793-5, 8vo, 3 vols.

Hare, Augustus J. C. Epitaphs for Country Churchyards, Collected and Arranged. Oxford: Parker and Co., 1856, 12mo., 70 pp.

Harrison, Rev. F. Bayford, Churchyard Poetry, *Macmillan's Magazine*, vol. 47, pp. 296-302.

Henney, William, of Hammersmith. A New and Improved Edition of Moral and Interesting Epitaphs, and Remarkable Monumental Inscriptions in England and America, to which are added Poems on Life, Death, and Eternity. Printed for and sold only by the Editor. Ninth edition, with additions, n.d., 8vo, 60 pp.; another edition, 1814, 12mo.

Hervey, James, M.A. Meditations among the Tombs. In a Letter to a Lady. *Meditations and Contemplations*, 1779, 8vo, 2 vols., vol 1, pp. 1-112.

Huddersford, George, M.A. The Uricamical Chaplet, a Selection of Original Poetry; comprising smaller Poems, Serious and Comic, Classical Trifles, Sonnets, Inscriptions and Epitaphs, Songs and Ballads, Mock-Heroic Epigrams, Fragments, &c. London, 1805, 8vo.

Inscriptions upon the Tombs and Gravestones in the Dissenters' Burial Place, near Bunhill Fields. London, 1717, 8vo.

J., W. Illustrated Guide to Kensal Green Cemetery. London, 1861, 8vo.

[James, J. A.] Bunhill Memorials; Sacred Reminiscences of three hundred Ministers and other Persons of note who are buried in Bunhill Fields, of every Denomination, with the Inscriptions on their Tombs and Gravestones. 1849, 8vo.

Jones, James, Gent. Sepulchrorum Inscriptiones: or, a Curious Collection of above Nine Hundred of the most Remarkable Epitaphs, Antient and Modern, Serious and Merry; In the Kingdoms of Great Britain, Ireland, &c. In English Verse. Faithfully collected. Westminster, 1727, 8vo.

Johnson, Samuel, LL.D. An Essay on Epitaphs. *Gentleman's Magazine*, vol. 10, pp. 593-596. Also included in his Works, Edited by Arthur Murphy, 1792, 12 vols., 8vo, vol. ii, pp. 270-280.

Essay on Pope's Epitaphs. "Lives of the Most Eminent Poets." [1801], vol. 3, pp. 199-217.

This Essay was first contributed to *The Universal Visitor*, and afterwards included in the "Lives of the Poets," where it is placed at the end of the Life of Pope, and is reprinted in the "Works of Dr. Johnson," [vol. xi, pp. 199-216].

Kelke, W. H. Churchyard Manual, with Five Hundred Epitaphs. London, Cox, 1854, 8vo.

Kensal Green, The Cemetery at, the Grounds and Monuments, with a Memoir of the Duke of Sussex, n.d, 8vo, with illustrations.

Kippax, J. R. Churchyard Literature: Choice Collection of American Epitaphs. Chicago, 1876, 12mo.

Last Homes of the Londoners, *Chambers's Journal*, vol. 37, pp. 406-408.

Loaring, Henry James. Epitaphs: Quaint, Curious, and Elegant. With Remarks on the Obsequies of Various Nations. Compiled and Collated. London: William Tegg, n.d. [1872], 8vo, pp. vi-262.

M'Dowall, William. Memorials of St. Michael's, the Old Parish Churchyard of Dumfries, 1876, 8vo, pp. ix-446. [With a frontispiece (St. Michael's Church and Churchyard) and vignette title].

This is a most valuable local work.

Macgregor, Major Robert Guthrie, of the Bengal Retired List. Epitaphs from the Greek Anthology. Translated. London: Nissen and Parker, 1857, 8vo, 230 pp.

Macrae, D. Queer Epitaphs. Book of Blunders. London: Simpkin, Marshall, and Co., 1872.

Maitland, Charles, M.D. The Church in the Catacombs: a Description of the Primitive Church of Rome, Illustrated by its Sepulchral Remains. London: Longman, Brown, Green, and Longman. 1846, 8vo, 312 pp., with illustrations.
Chapter III. of this work gives an interesting account of the Catacombs as a Christian Cemetery.

Memorials of the Dead, The Journal of the Society for Preserving the, in the Churches and Churchyards of Great Britain. Norwich: Samuel Sayer, 1883, 8vo, Nos. 1—4. (continued).
A Quarterly Magazine of twenty-four pages.

Mills, J., of Cowbit, Lincolnshire. Verses, Odes, &c., on Spalding, and Letters and Epitaphs, addressed to various persons and subjects. n.d., 4to, 42 pp.

Monteith, Robert, M.A. A Theatre of Mortality: or, the Illustrious Inscriptions extant upon the Monuments in the Grey Friars' Church Yard, &c., in Edinburgh and its Suburbs. Edinburgh, 1704.
A Further Collection of Funeral Inscriptions over Scotland. Edinburgh, 1713, small 8vo, 2 vols.

Neve, John Le. Monumenta Anglicana: being Inscriptions on the Monuments of several Eminent Persons. London, 1717-19, 8vo, 5 vols.
Lives, The, Characters, Deaths, Burials and Epitaphs, &c., of all the Protestant Bishops of the Church of England, since the Reformation as settled by Queen Elizabeth, A.D., 1559. London, 1731, 8vo, vol. 1, in two parts; part 1, 268 pp., part 2, 288 pp.

Norfolk, Horatio Edward. Gleanings in Graveyards: a Collection of Curious Epitaphs. London: J. R. Smith, 1861, 12mo., 172 pp.; Second edition, 1861, 12mo., 172 pp.; Third edition, revised and enlarged, 1866, 12mo., 228 pp.

Northend, Charles. A Book of Epitaphs. New York, 1873, 12mo., 171 pp.

Norwood Cemetery, a Descriptive Sketch, with Copies of the Inscriptions, etc., 1847, 8vo, 42 pp., with many cuts.

Orchard, R. A New Selection of Epitaphs and Remarkable Monumental Inscriptions. Second edit., 1827, 12mo.

Parr, Samuel, D.D. Latin Inscriptions, *Works, Edited by J. Johnstone, M.D.*, vol. iv, pp. 559-655; English Inscriptions, ib. pp. 656-676; Illustrations of the Preceding Inscriptions, ib. pp. 677-720; and Correspondence Illustrative of the Inscriptions, vol. viii., pp. 555-656.

Parish Minister, A, Verses for Graves Stones in Churchyards. London, 1816, 8vo.

Parsons, Rev. Philip, M.A. The Monuments and Painted Glass of upwards of one hundred Churches, chiefly in the Eastern Part of Kent; most of which were examined by the Editor in person, and the rest communicated by the resident clergy. With an Appendix, containing three Churches in other counties [Hadleigh and Lavenham, Suffolk, and Dedham, Essex.] To which is added a small Collection of detached Epitaphs, with a few notes on the whole. Canterbury, 1794, 4to, pp. viii-549, with errata and indexes, 4 pages, pp. 424-8, omitted.

Mr. Parsons died at the College, at Wye, in 1812, at the age of eighty-three.

Peck, Francis, M.A. Desiderata Curiosa: or, a Collection of Divers Scarce and Curious Pieces relating chiefly to Matters of English History; consisting of Choice Tracts, Memoirs, Letters, Wills, Epitaphs, &c. Transcribed, many of them, from the originals themselves, and the rest from divers Ancient MS. copies, or the MS. Collections of

Sundry Famous Antiquaries and other Eminent Persons, both of the last and present Age. The whole as far as possible digested into an order of time, and illustrated with ample Notes, Contents, Additional Discourses, and a complete Index. Adorned with cuts. A new edition, greatly corrected, with some Memoirs of the Life and Writing of Mr. Peck. London: Printed for Thomas Evans in the Strand, MDCCLXXIX., 2 vols., 4to. [With portrait and nine plates.]

Peirse, C. G. B. Riddles, Epitaphs, and Bon Mots. Designed by C. Grace, 1873, 4to.

Pettigrew, Thomas Joseph, F.R.S., F.S.A. Chronicles of the Tombs. A Select Collection of Epitaphs, Preceded by an Essay on Epitaphs and other Monumental Inscriptions, with Incidental Observations on Sepulchral Antiquities. (Bohn's Antiq. Lib.,) 1857, 8vo, pp. v-529.

Pope, Alexander, Epitaphs on Charles, Earl of Dorset; Sir William Trumbal; Hon. S. Harcourt; James Craggs; Nicholas Rowe; Mrs. Corbet; Hon. Robert and Mary Digby; Sir G. Kneller; Gen. Henry Withers; Elijah Fenton; Mr. Gay; Sir I. Newton; F. Atterbury, D.D.; Edmund, Duke of Buckingham. *Works, edited by Bishop Warburton*, 1770, 8vo, 9 vols. Vol. vi, pp. 85-103.

Preparing for the End. *Chambers's Journal*, vol. 49, pp. 229-232.

Pulleyn, William, Church-Yard Gleanings and Epigrams. London, n.d., [1830] 12mo.

[Ranken, Peter]. Epitaphs: or, Church-yard Gleanings. " Better to have a bad Epitaph when dead, than their ill report while living."—*Hamlet*. Collected by Old Mortality, jun. London: Bemrose and Sons, and Ranken and Co. n.d. [1874] 8vo, 184 pp.

Richings, Benjamin. Original and Selected Epitaphs, with Essays. London: Parker and Son, 1840, post 8vo.

Robinson, Joseph R., Sculptor, Derby. Epitaphs, Collected from the Cemeteries of London, Edinburgh, Glasgow, Hull, Leicester, Sheffield, Manchester, Nottingham, Birmingham, Derby, &c. With Original and Selected Epitaphs by Tennyson, Longfellow, Montgomery, Mrs. Hemans, Eliza Cook, Wordsworth, Robert Nicholl, Chas. Mackay, Milman, Mrs. Norton, J. B. Langley, Mrs. Sigourney, Mrs. Barbauld, Bernard, G. W. Longstaff, Alaric Watts, &c. The whole collected and arranged. London, Atchley, 1859, 12mo., 208 pp.

Rogers, Rev. Charles, LL.D. Monuments and Monumental Inscriptions in Scotland. Printed for the Grampian Club, 1871, 8vo, 2 vols.

"Dr. Rogers has not merely collected the epitaphs and inscriptions on the tombstones and monuments of Scotland, but he often gives illustrative particulars of a biographical and historical character. For this and similar things, his work must become a standard book of reference."—*Glasgow Star.*

S., H. L., and L. S. M. Epitaphs collected from Holy Writ, and our best Authors on Sacred Subjects. Arranged and edited by G. B. Chaloner. London: Atchley, 1868, 12mo. 200 pp.

Sanderson, Robert. Lincoln Cathedral; an exact copy of all the Ancient Monumental Inscriptions there, as they stood in MDCXLI; collected. And compared with and corrected by Sir William Dugdale's MS. Survey. London, 1851, 8vo.

Simpson, Joseph. A Collection of Curious, Interesting, and Facetious Epitaphs, Monumental Inscriptions, &c. London: Published and sold by Joseph Simpson; 1854, 8vo, 48 pp.

BIBLIOGRAPHY OF EPITAPHS. 171

Smart, Christopher. Poems on Several Occasions, viz., Munificence and Modesty; Female Dignity; To Lady Hussey Delaval; Verses from Catullus; After Dining with Mr. Murray; Epitaphs; &c. London, 1763, 4to.

Smith, W. Browning. Epitaph. *Encyclopædia Brit.*, ninth edition, vol. viii, pp. 493-496.

Snow, J. Lyra Memorialis; Original Epitaphs, &c.. with an Essay by William Wordsworth. London: Bell, 1847, 12mo.

This is a second and an enlarged edition of his *Light in Darkness: Churchyard Thoughts*, which was published in 1844.

Tissington, Silvester. A Collection of Epitaphs and Monumental Inscriptions on the most Illustrious Persons of all Ages and Countries; 1857, 8vo, 530 pp.

Toldervy, William. Select Epitaphs. London: Owen, 1755, 8vo, 2 vols.

Tombs, Among the. *Household Words*, vol. 17, pp. 372-375.

Tombstones, Inscriptions on. *Christian Remembrancer*, vol. 6, pp. 421.

Trowsdale, Thomas Broadbent, F.R.H.S. A Visit to the Old Burial Ground in Castle Street, Hull. Hull: Printed and Published by J. M. Taylor, 1878, 8vo, 8 pp.

Reprinted from *The Hull Miscellany*.

Wake, H. T. All the Monumental Inscriptions in the graveyards of Brigham and Bridekirk, near Cockermouth, in the County of Cumberland, from 1666 to 1876. Cockermouth, 1878, 8vo.

Walker, G. A., Surgeon. Gatherings from Grave Yards. Particularly those of London: With a concise History of the Modes of Interment Among different Nations, from the earliest periods. And a Detail of dangerous and fatal results produced by the unwise and revolting custom of inhuming the Dead in the midst of the Living. London : Longman and Co.; Nottingham, J. Hicklin ; 1839, 8vo, pp. xvii-258. [With an engraved title.]

Webb, T. A New Select Collection of Epitaphs: Panegyrical and Moral, Humorous, Whimsical, Satyrical, and Inscriptive. London, 1775, 12mo., 2 vols.

Weever, John. Ancient Funerall Monuments within the United Monarchie of Great Britaine, Ireland, and the Ilands adiacent, with the dissolved Monasteries therein contained ; their Founders, and what eminent persons have beene in the same interred ; As also the Death and buriall of certaine of the Bloud Roiall, the Nobilitie, and Gentrie of these Kingdomes entombed in forraine Nations, with other matters mentioned in the insuing Title. Composed by the Travels and Studie of John Weever. Spe labor leuis. London : Printed by Tho: Harper, MDCXXXI. And are to be sold in Little Britayne by Laurence Sadler at the signe of the Golden Lion. Fol., 871 pp. [With Portrait and Engraved Title.]

Westminster Abbey, The History and Antiquities of, and Henry VII's Chapel ; their Tombs, Ancient Monuments, and Inscriptions, &c. Illustrated. London, 1856, 4to.

Wignell, J. A Collection of Original Pieces : consisting of Poems, Prologues, Epilogues, Songs, Epistles, Epitaphs, &c. London, 1762, 8vo.

Winchester Cathedral. Historical and Critical Account of, with a review of the Monuments ; 1801, 8vo, 148 pp.

Index.

Abdidge, John, 37.
Abel, John, 155.
Aberfeldy, Perthshire, 75.
Abesford, 63.
Adams, John, 39.
Adams's, W. Davenport, " Dict. of Eng. Literature," quoted, 136.
Adlington, 63, 64.
Aliscombe, Devon., 45.
Andrews's, W., "Historic Romance," quoted, 101.
Anne, Queen, 76.
Appleby, H. C., quoted, 128.
Ardwick Cemetery, 98.
Ashburton, 151.
Ashford, Mr., 139.
——, Mary, Booker's epitaph on, 138.
Ashover, Derby., 94.
Audley's *Companion to the Almanac*, quoted, 62.
Ault Hucknall, Derby., 22.
Axon's, W. E. A., " Lancashire Gleanings," quoted, 137.
Aylesbury, 39.
BACCHANALIAN EPITAPHS, 54.
Bagshaw, Samuel, 46.
Bakers, Company of, 50.
Bakewell, Derby., 3-6, 133, 152. Church, 3, 4.
Ball's, H. W. " The Social Hist. and Antiqs. of Barton-on-Humber," quoted, 147.
Barbadoes, 36.
Barber, John, 127.

Bardesley's, Rev. C. W. " Memorials of St. Anne's Church, Manchester," quoted, 53.
Barker, Christopher, 19.
Barnstaple, 89.
Barrow-on-Soar, Leicester., 88.
Barton-on-Humber, 146-148; Ball's " Social Hist. and Antiqs. of," quoted, 147 ; King's Head Public House, 148 ; St. Peter's Churchyard, 146.
Barwick-in-Elmet, Yorks., 76.
Baskerville, John, 18.
Bath, 96 ; Cathedral 97.
Battersea, 67 ; The Church at, 67.
Battle, Sussex, Collection of Smoke money in, 61.
Becke, Rev. John, 86.
Beckley, 100.
Bede, Cuthbert, see Bradley, Rev. E., B.A.
Belbroughton, Worcester., 7, 8; The Church at, 71.
Bellem, Worcester. 7.
Bellow, J, F., 116.
Benson, Miss, 109.
Berkely, Gloucester., 35.
Berkshire, 131, 132.
Beverley, Yorks., 98, 116; The Minster, 69, 91 ; St. Mary's Church, 98 ; Tablet of two Danish Soldiers at, 116.
Biffin, Sarah, 124, 125 ; see also Wright, Mrs.
Billinge, William, 65.
Bingley, 11.

INDEX.

Bingham, Notts., 3.
Birmingham, 19.
Birstal, 26.
Blackett, John, 48.
Bletchley, 89.
Blidworth, 26-28; Archer's Water, 27; Forest, 29.
Blidworth Rocking, 26, 28.
Bloodworth, Sarah, see Dale, Sarah.
Bodger, Samuel, 68.
Bolsover, Derby., 35.
Bolton Lancashire, 120, 121.
——, Yorks., 112.
Booker, Dr, epitaph on Mary Ashford, 138.
Booth, Hannah, 92, 93.
——, John, 92, 93.
——, Tom, 24, 25.
Bowes, Yorks., 145.
Bradbury, Thomas, 139, 140.
——, William, 139, 140.
Bradley, Rev. E., B.A., (Cuthbert Bede), quoted, 7.
——, W., the Yorkshire Giant, 121, 122.
Breighmet, 121.
Bremhill, Wiltshire, 66.
Briscoe's, John D., "Hist. of Bolton," quoted, 120, 121.
——, J. Potter, 59, 141; 'Nottinghamshire Facts and Fictions" quoted, 59.
Bridgeford-on-the-Hill, Notts., 37.
Bridgnorth, 21.
Briggs, Hezekiah, 11.
Brighton, 70, 73; Churchyard, 70; Marine Parade, 73.
Bristol, 50.
Broadbent, John, 12.
Broomsgrove, 38.
Brown's, C., "Annals of Newark-upon-Trent," quoted, 130.
Buck, J., 102, 105.
Buckett, John, 56, 57.
Buller, Rev. H., 39.

Bullingham, 45.
Bunney, 29.
Burbage, Rich., 107.
Burkitt, Jonathan, 147, 148.
Burns's, Robert, epitaph on John Dove, 58.
Burton, 144
—— Joyce, 151.
Bury St. Edmunds, Suffolk, 17, 69, 150.
Butler, Samuel, 98.
——, Samuel, author of "Hudibras," 125, 126; O'Brien's epitaph on, 125; Wesley's epigram on, 126.
——, Samuel W., 98, 99.
Buttress, Jas. Epps, 79.
Byfleet, 105.
Byng, Admiral, 77, 78.
Byrne, Simon, 30.
Byron's, Lord, epitaph on John Adams, 39; on John Blackett, 48.
Bywater, Ann, 60.
——, John, 60.
——, John, son of above, 60.
Cadman, a famous "flyer," 101.
Callow, Rev. William, 8.
Campbell, Capt. Patrick, 75.
Carlyle, Thomas, 80.
Carmichael, Capt. James, 72.
Caroline, Queen, 105.
Carter, S., 30.
Cartwright, Henry, 23.
Castleton, Derby., 154.
Catherine, Queen of Henry VIII., 10.
Cave, ——, 88.
——, Edward, sen., 42.
——, Edward, jun., 42.
——, Jos., 42.
——, William, 42.
Cave, South, 140.
Caxton, William, 14.
Chapman's Dr. Thos., epitaph on Henry Jenkins, 112.

Chambers's, Dr. Robert, "Book of Days," quoted, 9, 10, 101, 105 ; "Dom. Annals of Scotland," quoted 114.
Chambers's Journal, quoted, 111.
Charles I., 113, 114, 128, 131.
—— II., 67, 113, 114, 133 ; and Butler's "Hudibras," 126.
Charlton, John, 21.
Chatham, 59.
Checkley, Stafford., 85.
Chelsea Hospital, 66, 73.
Chepstow, Monmouth., 130-133 ; Castle, 131, 133 ; Church, 132.
Cheshire, 111.
Chest, Rev. —., 132. Downton's epitaph on, 132.
Chester, 45.
Chesterfield, Lord, 17.
Chimney Money, see Smoke Money.
Chiswick, 97.
Clay, Hercules, 128, 129.
——, John, 63.
——, Mary, 63.
——, Thomas, 63, 64.
Cleater, S,. 152.
Clemetshaw, Henry, 91.
Cliff, Elizabeth, 151.
Clifton, Gloucester., 97.
Clockmakers, The Company of, and the restoration of Harrison's tomb at Hampstead, 36.
Cocks, Rev. Chas. S., 8.
Cole, William, Dean of Lincoln, 87, 88.
Collison, David, 81.
Colton, Stafford., 46.
Corby, Lincoln., 50.
Corser, Annie, 134.
——, Henry, 134.
Corsica, Theodore, King of, 135.
Cotton, Rev. John, 16.
Coventry, 20 ; St. Michael's Churchyard, 20, 29. 31.
Coventry Mercury, quoted, 20.

Crackles, Thomas, 80.
Crayford, 1.
Creton, 151.
Crich, Derby., 43.
Crompton, Jas.. 121.
——, Mary, 121.
Cromwell, Oliver, 113, 132.
Cruker, John, 48.
Culloden, 110.
Dale, Elizabeth, (neé Foljambe), 133.
——, John, 133, 134.
——, Sarah, (neé Bloodworth) 133, 134.
Danish Soldiers, Tablet of the, at Beverley, 116, 119.
Darfield, Barnsley, 155.
Darlington, 13.
Darnbrough, William, 11, 12.
Darneth, Dartford, 59.
Dart, Rose, 89.
Dartmoor, 33.
Dartmouth, 76.
Davidson, Lieut. Alex., 78.
——, Harriet, 78.
Day, William, 86.
Deal, 78.
Deans, Jeannie, 27.
Defoe's, Daniel, "Robinson Crusoe," quoted, 136.
Delamoth, Mrs. Jane, 153.
Depledge, Thos., 156.
Dibdin, Rev. T. F., D.D., quoted, 10.
Dickinson, Mr., 110.
Dinsdale's, Dr. F., F.S.A., "Ballads and Songs of David Mallet," quoted, 146.
Dixon, George. 22.
Dove, John, 58.
Downton's epitaph on Rev. —., Chest, 132.
Dublin, 16.
Duck, S., 102, 105, 106 ; Swift's epigram on, 105.
Dudley, Worcester, 138.

INDEX.

Dundas, Lord, 108.
Dunton, Bucks., 39.
Eakring, Notts., 23.
Easton, William, 80.
Ecclesfield Churchyard, 23.
Edinburgh, 17, 27.
Edmonds, John, 77.
Edwalton, 59.
Edward VI., 113.
Elizabeth, Queen, 19, 113, 114.
Ellenborough, Lord, 139.
Empedocles, quoted, 84.
EPITAPHS, BACCHANALIAN, 54;
  Miscellaneous, 150; Punning,
  84; Typographical, 14; On
  Actors and Musicians, 90;
  Bakers, 49, 50; A Blacksmith,
  43; Booksellers, 40-42; A
  Builder, 45; Carpenters, 46,
  50; Carriers, 39; A Coach-
  man, 39; A Dyer, 47; En-
  gineers, 37-38; Gardeners,
  51-52; A Mason, 46; Musi-
  cians and Actors, 90; Notable
  Persons, 108; Parish Clerks,
  1; Potters, 44-5; Publicans,
  54-56; Sailors and Soldiers,
  65; Sextons and Parish Clerks,
  1; Shoemakers, 48; Soldiers
  and Sailors, 65; Sportsmen,
  21; Tradesmen, 33; Watch-
  makers, 33-37; Weavers, 47.
Eton, 60.
Evans's, John, "Life of S. W.
  Butler," quoted, 99.
Eyre and Spottiswood, printers, 19
——, Vincent, 141, 142; Briscoe's
  account of, 141.
Falkirk, Scotland, 110.
Faulder, George, alderman and
  printer of Dublin, 16, 17.
Fawfield Head, Stafford., 65.
Ferrensby, 111.
Field, Joseph, 84, 85.
——, Theophilus, 85.
FitzHerbert, Ralph, 7.

FitzOsborne, William, 7.
Flamborough Head, 82.
Flixton, Lancash., 92.
Flockton, Thos., 12, 13.
Foljambe, Elizabeth, see Dale,
  Elizabeth.
Folkestone, Kent, 61.
Fort William Cemetery, 75.
Fotheringay, 11.
Foulby, Yorks., 36.
Fountain Dale Cross, 28.
Fox, Henry. 47.
Franklin, Dr. Benjamin, 15, 16.
——, Deborah, 16.
Freland, Mrs. 59.
Garrick, David, 96; Epitaph on
  William Hogarth, 97, 98; on
  Jas. Quin, 97.
Gedge, L., 17.
Gentleman's Magazine, quoted, 5, 6,
  42, 115.
George II., 105.
—— III., 125.
—— IV., 70.
Germany, 121.
Gibraltar, 73.
Gillingham, 99.
Gloucester, 57.
Gloucester Notes and Queries, quoted,
  136.
Gloucestershire, 127; St. Peter
  Abbey, 128.
Goëthe, J. W., quoted, 80.
Golding, Samuel, 73.
——, Phœbe, see Hessel.
Goldsmith, Thos., 76.
Grainge's, William, "Yorkshire
  Longevity," quoted. 111.
Grantham, Lincoln., 147-148.
Gray, Catherine, 45.
——, Robert, 49; his Hospital, 49.
Greenfield, 139.
Greenwich, Kent, 56; The Pig
  and Whistle Public House, 56
Griffiths, Geo., 68.

INDEX. 177

Grindon, Stafford., 156.
Guardian, The, quoted, 87.
Guy, John, 127.
Hackett, Robert, 22.
Haddon Hall, Derby., 5.
Haigh, Brian, 152.
——, John, 152.
——, Martha, 152.
Hall, Micah, 154.
Hamilton, 83
Hampstead, Middx., 35.
Hampsthwaite, Yorks., 122.
Hanslope, Bucks., 30.
Harding-Booth, 46.
Hardwick Park, 22.
Harrison, John, the Inventor, 36.
——, William, 81.
Harrogate, 109-111.
Hart, Thomas, 3.
Hartwith Chapel, Nidderdale, 11.
Haselton, Mary. 150.
Hawksworth's, Dr., epitaph on Joseph Cave, 42.
Hayley, W., 43.
Henry VII., 113.
—— VIII., 7, 113.
Hereford, 85, 155; Cathedral, 85.
Hessel, Phœbe, 70-75.
Hessle, Hull, 47.
Heywood, John, 46.
Highgate Cemetery 30.
Hill, Otwell, D.D., 87.
Hilton Castle, Durham, 101.
Hilton's John, Fool, 101.
Hinde, Thomas, 35.
Hippisley, John, 97.
Hiseland, William, 66.
Hobson, —, University Carrier, 39-40.
Hogarth, William, 97, 98, 101; Garrick's epitaph on, 97, 98.
Horncastle, 83.
Hornsea, 86.
Howard, John, 53.
Hughenden Churchyard, 127.
Hulm, John, 20.

Hurtle, F., 8.
Hull, 60, 80, 84, 116, 119, 140; Castle Street Burial Ground, 60; Field, Jos., twice mayor of, 84, 85; Hessle Road Cemetery, 80; Holy Trinity Church, 84, 91; St. Mary's Church, Sculcoates, 153.
Hythe Churchyard, Kent; epitaph on a Fishmonger in, 32.
Indies, East, 73.
Indies, West, 73.
Inglott, William, 90.
Ireland, 121.
Isnell, Peter, 1, 2.
Jackson, Thos., 100.
James I., 113, 132.
Jenkins, Henry, 112, 113; Dr. Chapman's epitaph on, 112-113.
Jerrold's, D., epitaph on Chas. Knight, 107.
Jewitt, Llewellynn, F.S.A., quoted, 3.
Jobling, Mrs. C., 124.
Jones, Edward, printer, 14, 15.
——, John, 128.
Joy, Richard, "Kentish Samson," 123.
Juan Fernandez, Island of, 135.
Kettlethorpe, Lincoln., 86.
Kew, Surrey, 105.
Kimbolton Castle, Huntingdon, 10
Kingston, Duke of, 23.
Kirk Hallam, Derby., 152.
Knaresborough, 108, 109, 110; Blind Jack of, 108-111.
Knight, Chas., Jerrold's epitaph on, 107.
Knighton, South Wales, 155.
Lackington, James, 41.
Lambert, Daniel, the Lincolnshire Giant, 122, 123.
——, Geo., 91.
Lambeth, 52.
Lancashire, 111.

A A

Largo, Fife, 135.
Leake, Thomas, 26-29.
Leeds, 12.
Leek, Stafford., 156.
Leen, river, 24.
Leicester, 122.
Leominster, 155.
Lillyard, Miss, 116.
Lillyard's Edge, Battle of, 115.
Lillington, Dorset., 87.
Lillywhite, the Cricketer, 30.
Lincoln, 87 ; Cathedral, 87.
Lincolnshire, 142, 143.
Lisbon, 36.
Liverpool, 55. 124 ; St. James's Cemetery, 124.
Llandaff, South Wales, 85.
London, 27, 36, 39, 49, 57, 62, 101, 114, 121, 126, 127 ; Boar's Head Tavern, Great Eastcheap, 62 ; Covent Garden Churchyard, epitaph of John Taylor, the Water Poet in, 57 ; King's Bench Prison, 135 ; King's College Hospital, 102 ; Phœnix Alley, 57 ; Portugal Street, 101 ; Red Lion Square, 36; St. Anne's Church yard, Soho, 134 ; St. Clement Danes Burial ground, 101; St. Michael's Church, 62 ; St. Paul's Church, Covent Garden, 125 ; The Savoy. 14 ; Tothill Fields, 139 ; Westminster Abbey, 11, 14, 96, 126.
Longnor, Stafford , 46, 65.
Luton Churchyard, Bedford, 27.
Lydford, Dartmoor, 33.
Macbeth, John, 93, 94.
McKay, Sandy, the Scottish Giant, 30.
Malibran, Madame, 95.
Mallet's ballad of " Edwin and Emma," quoted, 145-146 ; "Ballads and Songs," quoted, 146.

Manchester, 110.
" Manchester Lit. Club Papers," quoted, 99.
Market Weighton, 121.
Marlborough, Duke of, 65.
Marten, Sir Henry, 132.
——, Henry, 131, 132, 133.
Martin, John, 51.
Mary, Queen, 113, 114.
Masham, Yorks., 122 ; Swinton Hall, 122.
Mauchline, Scotland, 58.
Mawer, Hannah, 148.
——, Rev. John, D.D., 148.
Maxton, Scotland, 116.
Medford, Grace, 89.
Merlin's Cave, Richmond Park, 105
Melton-Mowbray, Leicester., 61.
"Mercury Hawkers in Mourning, The," quoted, 15.
Merrett, Thos., 133.
Metcalf, John, Blind Jack of Knaresborough, 108-111.
Micklehurst, Chester, 60.
Middleditch, William, 69.
Middleton Tyas, Richmond, 148.
Miller, Joe, 101-105.
Mills, John, 21.
Minskip, 111.
Morgan, Meredith, 92.
Morley's Henry " Memoirs of Bartholomew Fair," quoted, 124-125.
Morton, Earl of, 124, 125.
Morville, Bridgnorth, 21.
Mottram, Chester, 21.
New Forest, Hants., Collection of Smoke Money in, 62.
Newark, Notts., 128, 129.
Newcastle-on-Tyne, 2 ; All Saints Church, 2.
Newhaven, Sussex, 54.
Newport, Monmouth., 93 ; Old Cemetery. The, 93.
Newton, George, 22.

Nidderdale, 11.
Norris, Admiral, 73.
Norwich, 90 ; Cathedral, 90.
Notes and Queries, quoted, 62.
Nottingham, 24 ; Park, 24 ; St. Nicholas' burial ground, 24.
"Nottingham Date Book," quoted, 24.
O'Brien's, Mr., epitaph on Samuel Butler, 125.
Ockham, Surrey, 50.
Okey, John, 121.
Ollerton, Notts., 55.
Orange, Prince of, 116.
Orford, H. Walpole, Earl of, 134.
Osborne, —, 7.
Ostler, Miss, 148.
Oxford, 48 ; Ashmolean Museum, 52.
Pady, James, 45.
Pannal, Yorks., 55.
PARISH CLERKS AND SEXTONS, EPITAPHS ON, 1.
Parker, —, engine-driver, 39.
Parkes, John, 29, 30.
Parkyns, Thomas, 29
Parr, Edward, 69.
Pateley Bridge Church registers 12
Pausanias, 84.
Pearce, Dickey, Dean Swift's epitaph on, 100.
——, General, 73.
Pegge, Rev. Samuel, 6.
Peirce, Thomas, watchmaker, 35.
Pennecuik's, Alex., epitaph on Marjory Scott, 114, 115.
Peterborough, Northampton, 9, 88 ; Cathedral, 9, 88.
Pettigrew's, T. J., "Chronicles of the Tombs," quoted, 61.
Philadelphia, Christ Church, 16.
Phillpot, Geo., 79.
Pickering, Robert, 81.
Pickford, Rev. John, M.A., on the death of two Danish Soldiers at Beverley, 116.

Plumtree, John, 141.
Plymouth, Devon., 73.
Pope, Alex., 106.
Portsmouth, Hants., 78.
Portugal, 51.
——, Don John Emanuel, King of, 51 ; Martin, John, his natural son, 51.
Preston, Lancash., 136.
——, Richard, 13.
——, Robert, waiter at the Boar's Head Tavern, London, 62.
Price, E. B., on restoration of Northampton Church, 62.
Prissick, Geo., 47.
Pritchard, Mrs., 96.
Pryme, A. de la, on the Danes, 119, 120.
PUNNING EPITAPHS, 84.
Putney, Surrey, 78.
Quantox Head, Somerset., 124.
Quin, Jas., Garrick's epitaph on, 97.
Railton, Martha, 145, 146.
Ramillies, 65.
Ratcliffe-on-Soar, 3.
Raw, Frank, 2.
Reader, Mr., 139.
Ridge, Thomas, 23.
Ridsdale, George, 122.
——, Isabella, 122.
——, Jane, the Yorkshire Dwarf, 122.
Roe, Charles, 4.
——, Dorothy, 4, 5.
——, Millicent, 4.
——, Philip, 6, 7.
——, Samuel, 4, 5, 6.
——, Sarah, wife of Samuel, 4.
——, Sarah, wife of Philip, 7.
Rogers, Rebecca, 61.
Rooke, Sir Geo., 65.
Ross's, F., F.R.H.S., "Celebrities of the Yorkshire Wolds," quoted, 121.
Rotherham, Yorks., 49.
Rothwell, Yorks., 12.

Routleigh, Geo., 33.
Rudder's, Samuel, "History of Gloucestershire," quoted, 136.
——, Roger, see Rutter.
Rugby, Warwick., 42.
Rutter, John, 136.
——, Roger, (*alias* Rudder), 136.
Saddleworth, Yorks., 12, 139.
St. David's, South Wales, 85.
Salisbury Wilts., 31
Salmond, Capt., 28.
Salterford, 28.
Sanderson's, Bp., "Survey of Lincoln Cathedral," quoted, 87.
Sands, Rev. Samuel, 148.
Sarnesfield, Weobley, 155.
Scarborough, 81.
Scarle, North, Lincoln., 69.
Scarlett, William, 9, 10.
Scatchard, Thomas, 140.
Scotland, 110, 114, 115, 135.
Scots, Mary, Queen of, 11.
Scott, John, 55.
——, Marjory, 114; Alex. Pennecuik's epitaph on, 114, 115.
——, Sir W., "Tales of a Grandfather," quoted, 115; "Anne of Geierstein," quoted, 119.
Scrope, Capt. Gervase, 31.
——, family, of Bolton, Yorks., 31.
Seaham, Durham, 48.
Selby, Yorks., 2, 77.
Selkirk, Alex., 135, 136.
Shakespeare, William, 96, 97, 107.
Sheahan's J. J., "Hist. of Hull," quoted, 153.
Sheffield, 40; Trinity Churchyard, 40.
Short-hand, Inscription in, in St. Mary's Church, Sculcoates, Hull, 153.
Shrewsbury, 101; St. Julian's Church, 134; St. Mary Friars, 101.
Shullcross, P., 154.
Silkstone, Yorks., 44.

Simpson, Jeremiah, 140.
Slater, Joseph, watchmaker, 34.
Sleaford, Lincoln., 47.
Smith, Isaac, 68.
——. Robert, 3; Richard, 40.
Smoke Money, or Chimney Money, Collection of, in Battle, and the New Forest, 61, 62.
Southam, Warwick., 148; Church, 148.
South-Hill, Bedford., 77.
Southwell, Notts., 39.
Spalding, Joseph, 76.
Sparke, Mrs. Rose, 89.
Spectator, The, quoted, 30, 78.
Spencer, Earl, K.G., President of the Roxburghe Club, 14.
Spofforth, Yorks., 108, 111.
Spong, see Sprong.
Sportive Wit: The Muses' Merriment, quoted, 57.
SPORTSMEN, EPITAPHS ON, 21.
Spottiswood, Eyre &, printers, 19.
Sprong, John, 50.
Stalybridge, 22.
Stamford, Lincoln., 122.
St. Martin's Church, 122, 123.
Stockbridge, Hants., 56; King's Head Inn, 65.
Stockport, Chester., 111.
Stokes, Thomas, "Dumb Tom," 144.
Stoney Middleton, 95.
Straker, Daniel, 116.
Street, Amos, 25, 26.
Strutt, Matthew, 152.
Suffolk, Earl of, 100.
Sutherland, Duke of, 93.
Sutton Coldfield, Warwick., 137.
Swain's, Charles, epitaph on S. W. Butler, 99.
Swift's, Dean, 17, 100, 105; epigram on S. Duck, 105, 106; epitaph on Dickey Pearce, 100.
——, George, 95.

INDEX.

Swift, —, 95.
——, Margaret, 95.
Taunton, Somerset., 49.
Tawton, Devon., 89.
Taylor, Hannah, 44.
——, John, 44.
——, John, The Water Poet, 57, 58.
Teanby, W., 142, 143.
Teetotal ; W. E. A. Axon, on the origin of the word, 137; R. Turner, author of the word, 137.
Tennis Ball, introduced in an epitaph, 31.
Tewkesbury, Gloucester., 133 ; Abbey, 133.
Thackerey, Joseph, 55.
Thanet, Isle of, 123 ; St. Peter's Churchyard, 123.
Thetcher. Thomas, 64.
Thompson, Francis, 55.
Thornton, A., 138, 139.
——, Col., 110.
Thorsby on Tom Booth's exploits, 24.
Tideswell, Derby., 152.
Tiffey, Jack, 89.
Times, The, quoted, 35.
Tipper, Thomas, 54.
Tonbridge, see Tunbridge
Tonson, Jacob, printer and bookseller, 15.
Tradescent. John, 52.
Tradescants, 52.
Trowsdale, T. B., F.R.H.S., quoted, 130-133.
Tunbridge Wells, (Tonbridge) 59.
Turar, Thomas, 50.
Turner, Richard, 136, 137 ; author of the word " Teetotal," 137.
Turpin, Dick, 27.
TYPOGRAPHICAL EPITAPHS, 14.
Uley, Gloucester., 136.
Upton-on-Severn, 56.
Uttoxeter, Stafford., 34 ; Churchyard, 34.

Wakefield, 90.
Wales, 92.
Walford, Edward, M.A., quoted, 35, 36.
Walker, Ann, 37.
——, Benjamin, 37.
——, John, 37 ; William, 82.
Wall, David, 94.
Wallas, Robert, 2.
Warren, Borlase, 141.
Warwick, 137, 138.
Weem, Scotland, 75.
Welton, 140.
Wendesley tomb, 6.
Wesley's, S., epigram on Samuel Butler, 126.
Westminster Abbey, 11, 14, 96, 126.
Westminster, St. Margaret's Church, 14.
Weston, 47.
Whalley, Lancash., 137.
Whitehall, Rev. James, 85.
Whitaker's, T. D., LL.D., epitaph on John Wigglesworth, 137.
Whitsun Farthings, or Smoke Money, 62.
Whittaker, William, 77.
Whittington, Derby., 6.
Whitworth, Rev. R. H., quoted, 26.
Wigglesworth. John, Whitaker's epitaph on, 137.
William IV., 125.
William, Adam, printer, 17, 18.
Wimbledon. Surrey, 51.
Winchester, Hants., 64.
Wingfield, North, Derby., 63.
Winterton, 142 ; Church, the School in the vestry of, 142.
Wirksworth. Derby., 153.
Wolverley, Worcester., 8.
Woodbridge, Suffolk, 76.
Worme, Sir Richard, 88.
Worrall, James, 8
——, Thomas, 8.
Wright, Joe.

Wright, Mrs., (Sarah Biffin) 125.
Wrightson, Rodger, 145, 146.
Wycombe, High, Bucks., 37, 127.
Wynter, Sir Edward, 67, 68.
Yarmouth, 32, 47, 68; St. Nicholas' Church, 47.
York, 110, 151.
Yorkshire, 111, 145; Beverley, 98, 116; Bolton, 112; Bowes, 145; Darlington, 13; Ecclesfield, 23; Foulby, 36; Hampsthwaite, 122; Harrogate, 109. 111; Hartwith Chapel, 11;

Yorkshire, *continued*.
  Hessle, 47; Hornsea, 86; Knaresborough 108-110; Leeds, 12, 110; Market Weighton, 121; Masham, 122; Middleton Tyas, 148; Nidderdale, 11; Pannal, 55; Pateley,Bridge 12; Rotherham, 49; Rothwell, 12; Saddleworth, 12, 139; Scarborough, 81; Selby, 2; Sheffield, 40; Silkstone, 44; Spofforth, 108, 111; Wakefield, 90; Welton, 140.

Charles Henry Barnwell, Printer, 9, Savile Street, Hull.

WORKS BY WILLIAM ANDREWS, F.R.H.S.

HISTORIC ROMANCE.

Strange Stories, Characters, Scenes, Mysteries, and Memorable Events in the History of Old England.

In his present work Mr. Andrews has traversed a wider field than in his last book "Historic Yorkshire," but it is marked by the same painstaking care for accuracy, and also by the pleasant way in which he popularises strange stories and out-of-the-way scenes in English history. There is much to amuse in this volume as well as to instruct, and it is enriched with a copious index. — *Notes and Queries.*

A fascinating work.—*Whitehall Review.*

Mr. Andrews discourses about Ordeals, Forest Life and Laws, Guilds, Pledging in the Days of Yore, Skull Superstitions, Cure by Royal Touch, Fools and Jesters, Death Omens, and kindred topics in over a score of chapters, every one of which is as enthralling as a well-written novel. But Mr. Andrews' pages are instructive as well as entertaining, and he seems to have spared no pains to gather for us, from out-of-the-way corners and unknown sources, all kinds of much desired and welcome information.—*Newcastle Courant.*

Free by Parcels Post for Five Shillings.

HISTORIC YORKSHIRE.

Cuthbert Bede, the popular author of "Verdant Green," writing to *Society*, says: "Historic Yorkshire," by William Andrews, will be of great interest and value to everyone connected with England's largest county. Mr. Andrews not only writes with due enthusiasm for his subject, but has arranged and marshalled his facts and figures with great skill, and produced a thoroughly popular work that will be read eagerly and with advantage. This handsomely-bound, luxuriously-printed, and gilt-edged volume would, indeed, form a very appropriate school-gift, as well as a book to be placed on the library shelf of the student. A clear and copious index increases the value of a work that will be read with interest by the historian, the folk-lorist, the antiquary, and the lover of legendary lore.

Free by Parcels Post for Four Shillings.

CHAS. H. BARNWELL, 9, SAVILE STREET, HULL.

WORKS OF WILLIAM SMITH, F.S.A.S.

THREE WEEKS' TRIP TO FRANCE AND SWITZERLAND. Post 8vo., 100 pp. Published 1864. (F. Pitman)...... *Out of Print.*

Do. do. *Second Edition.* Crown 8vo, Published 1865. (W. H. Smith & Son, London) .... Do.

A YOKSHIREMAN'S TRIP TO ROME. Post 8vo. 200 pp. Published 1866. (Longmans)......... Do.

RAMBLES ABOUT MORLEY. Crown 8vo., Illustrated. 200 pp. Published 1866. (J. R. Smith.) Do.

HISTORY AND ANTIQUITIES OF MORLEY. Demy 8vo. Illustrated, 300 pp. Published 1876. (Longmans.) .... Do.

OLD YORKSHIRE. Vols. I., II., III., and IV., 1881-3. Demy 8vo. Profusely Illustrated. 320 pp. each. Published Yearly, in October. *s. d.* (Longmans.)............... *per vol.* 7 6
Do. do. Demy 4to .... ,, 15 0
Sold to Subscribers at the following prices :—
    Demy 8vo .... ,, 5 0
    Demy 4to .... ,, 10 6

*** Complete Sets of "OLD YORKSHIRE" to present date (Vols. 1 to 4) may be had for a short time, from the EDITOR, OSBORNE HOUSE, MORLEY. Sent carriage free on receipt of 25 0

WM. SMITH, OSBORNE HOUSE, MORLEY, NR. LEEDS.

www.ingramcontent.com/pod-product-compliance
Lightning Source LLC
Chambersburg PA
CBHW061322040426
42444CB00011B/2735